Growing Bromeliads

Growing Bromeliads

Edited by

**Barry E. Williams
and
Ian Hodgson**

CHRISTOPHER HELM
A & C Black · London

TIMBER PRESS
Portland, Oregon

This edition © 1990 Christopher Helm Publishers
First published by The Bromeliad Society of Australia, Inc. © 1988

Christopher Helm (Publishers) Ltd,
Imperial House, 21–25 North Street,
Bromley, Kent BR1 1SD

ISBN 0–7136–8069–5

Typeset by Florencetype Ltd, Kewstoke, Avon
Printed and bound in Great Britain by Biddles, Ltd.,
Guildford, Surrey

CONTENTS

Colour Plates

FIGURES

ACKNOWLEDGEMENTS

The editors are indebted to the following people, without whose contributions this book could not have been produced.

Chapters
Olwen Ferris   10
Grace Goode   11, 16
Valerie Hillman   8
Ian Hodgson   4
Clive Innes   2
Wayne Jeffery   3, 4, 14
Sabina Knees   2
Geoffrey Lawn   18
Bill Morris   2, 7
Cliff Norden   4
Joan Norden   6
Robert Reidl   1, 17
Ruby Ryde   5, 9, 15
Ellen Sloss   12
Ken Woods   13

Appendices
Joan Williams   5

Index
John Emery
Clive Innes

Colour Plates
Ken Woods
Fred Thompson

Illustrations
Valerie Hillman
Wayne Jeffery

Assistance
Richard Hargreaves
Elaine Jones

INTRODUCTION

This book was written by bromeliad enthusiasts for growers who are interested in the culture of plants which are unique, challenging and immensely interesting.

The aim has been to provide an insight into bromeliads from the viewpoint of the practical horticulturist, and whilst it is a modest attempt at being a text book on some aspects of bromeliads and their culture, it is not intended to be a scientific publication. This is not to say that the information contained is inaccurate, but that it is based upon the knowledge and experience of successful growers. As such, it should prove useful for the intended purpose.

We have endeavoured to include the main aspects of the habitats, growing conditions and culture of these remarkable plants, and dealt mainly with those genera which are commonly found in cultivation. To extend the coverage to include detailed discussion on all genera is beyond the realm of the book. However, for those who wish to extend their knowledge just a little further, a chapter providing brief notes on some of the more unusual genera is included.

As far as possible the use of scientific language has been avoided, but in quite a number of instances this has not been practical because it would have resulted in a loss of meaning. Wherever terminology is used which is not understood, a reference should be made to the glossary (Appendix 5). By and large the intelligent gardener should, we trust, not only understand the requirements of the Bromeliaceae but also, through practical culture, appreciate their beauty and diversity.

Due to this very diversity (and complexity), it was deemed unrealistic and unwise to attempt all-encompassing statements concerning growing conditions required by the Bromeliad family as a whole. The reason for this is that the natural habitats of various genera vary widely and appropriate consideration must be given to each of these in their cultivation. It is because of such considerations that this book treats each of the included genera separately, outlining its habitat, describing its appearance and growing conditions, and advising on the culture of some of its species. Each chapter dealing with a specific genus could therefore be regarded, to a certain extent, as standing alone.

However, for cultivation purposes it is helpful to note that various degrees of commonality can exist within sundry groupings of bromeliads (each of which can include a number of genera) concerning one or more of their individual requirements as to water and humidity, light, temperature or growing medium. This makes it possible for a number of species from different genera to be grown together under similar conditions, even though such conditions are not ideal in that they differ in various aspects from those of their individual habitats.

CHAPTER 1

ORIGIN, DISTRIBUTION AND ECOLOGY

Life is fascinating no matter where we meet it, but it seems to be nowhere more fascinating than where it is trying to come to terms with the often enormous stresses imposed by nature itself. The zones of high stress are the frontiers to life, but life forms which were endowed with the potential genetically to adapt and re-adapt have overcome these barriers, and have colonised in great diversity what could, on the surface, be considered a no-man's land for life.

It is usually plant life that has to conquer the hostile frontier before animal life can follow and sustain itself. Let us consider in this context examples such as the arid wastelands and deserts, and their multitude of drought-enduring cacti and succulents; the highly saline, oxygen-deficient mud flats along the shores of the warm oceans and their colonies of mangroves with salt-excreting organs in their leaves and aerial roots with which to breathe atmospheric oxygen at low tide; or the nutrient-impoverished swamps and bogs with their hosts of carnivorous plants which are able to flourish through compensating for the lack of nutrients in the soil by catching insects, which they digest to obtain vital minerals from their victims' bodies.

But possibly the most hostile, most unstable, most stressful of environments has been conquered by plants which have adapted to sustain themselves on barren rock or as epiphytes in the canopy of trees exposed to extremes of temperature, drought, intense sun, devastating rainstorms and to an extreme barrenness of nutrients; environments where plants are continuously threatened by dehydration, burning, dislodgement and starvation. Plants which colonise such harsh, forbidding habitats are notably orchids and bromeliads. The question arises: what mechanisms, what deviations from normal plant conventions have they employed to succeed in environments where more conventional plants would perish?

Bromeliads belong taxonomically to the angiosperms or flowering plants, the most advanced form of evolutionary development thus far attained by plants, which began to evolve about 200 million years ago at a time when the mammals also made their first appearance. As we know

1

from palaeontology, the flowering plants achieved dominance over more ancient plant groups such as mosses, ferns, cycads and conifers about 100 million years ago.

When flowering plants first evolved, the oceans of the southern hemisphere were dominated by a giant land mass referred to as Gondwanaland. This super-continent started to break up around 180 million years ago and its fragments drifted apart and are known today as the continents of Africa, Australia, Antarctica, South America and as the subcontinent of India. The latter, during its northward drift, collided with the northern hemisphere continent of Asia, forcing up the mountain range of the Himalayas.

Many flowering plants which had been well established on Gondwanaland prior to its break-up can still be found on two or more of the resulting continents; a notable example being the southern beech (*Nothofagus*) which has survived in south-eastern Australia and southern Chile, and is also known from fossil remains excavated in Antarctica.

Bomeliads must be considered to have evolved in South America after the break-up of Gondwanaland, as they are absent, with the exception of one species, from the other continents that once made up the giant land mass. From all that we know at present of the distribution of the bromeliad family, it seems that this group probably evolved in the Andean region of South America, for the greatest number of the more primitive types of the family are found in this particular area. From there they have radiated across most parts of South America, where they have found their present southern-most limit about 1000 km south of Buenos Aires and at around 44° south in Chile. When North and South America were joined by a land bridge they migrated across the isthmus of Panama into tropical and subtropical Central America and as far north as the south-east of Virginia in the United States.

The species *Pitcairnia feliciana* is the only bromeliad which is not native to the Americas. Its discovery in Guinea in West Africa was so unexpected that it was initially described in 1937, not as a pitcairnia, but as Willrussellia feliciana, a classification which related it to the lily family. The error was corrected one year later, but the mystery remained as to how this member of the bromeliad family ever crossed the Atlantic Ocean to reach Africa. Incidentally, the same mystery surrounds Rhipsalis cassutha, found in Africa and Madagascar, as it is the only species of cactus outside the Americas.

How long ago the ancestral archetype of bromeliads first evolved cannot be ascertained, but the oldest bromeliad-like fossil found in South American rock sediments has been dated as 30 million years old and has been named *Karatophyllum bromelioides*. One can conclude from this that the family Bromeliaceae is a relative newcomer in the plant kingdom which is reflected in the fact that it is made up of only about 2000 species.

This is a relatively small number when compared with such families as orchids or sunflowers which comprise about 15,000 species each.

But both orchids and sunflowers evolved much earlier than bromeliads; they occur today on all continents with the exception of Antarctica and therefore have had the necessary time, geographic dispersion and survival needs to adjust to a vastly greater number of environmental regimes. This has therefore resulted in a larger number of species than the Bromeliaceae, which has been basically restricted by geographic isolation to one continent and its more limited environmental and ecological challenges.

The approximately 2000 species which make up the family Bromeliaceae are divided into three subfamilies on the basis of genetic affinities: the Pitcairnioideae, Bromelioideae and Tillandsioideae which are all further subdivided into genera comprising the individual species. In round numbers both Pitcairnioideae and Bromelioideae have each a total of about 500 species, whereas the subfamily Tillandsioideae contains about 1000 species with the genus *Tillandsia* as the largest bromeliad genus accounting for almost 600 members. Although most bromeliad species share at least superficially a common design of appearance and survival strategy, it is the tillandsias which have evolved the greatest diversity of form, of nutrient procurement and of habitat tolerance. Apparently endowed with significantly greater genetic resilience and the power of broader adaptation than possibly inherent in other bromeliad genera, it comes as no surprise to find tillandsias as successful colonists in the widest range of available habitats.

The geographic distribution of bromeliads is by no means uniform. Areas with a particular abundance of species are Mexico, some regions of Central America, the West Indies, eastern and southern Brazil, and the Andean region from northern Chile to Colombia. The great tropical rainforests of the Amazon basin, on the other hand, are an area where bromeliads are unexpectedly scarce.

More bromeliads occur in moist mountain forest at between 1500 and 2500 m altitude than in any other habitat. If the postulation of an Andean origin of the family is correct, then perhaps too little evolutionary time has passed to allow its members to exploit such lowland habitats as Amazonia. Mountain regions richest in epiphytic bromeliads experience cloud envelopment for at least several hours every day throughout the year. Apparently, warm and temperate cloud forests with rather average annual rainfall provide the ideal habitat for many kinds of epiphytic plants. Here they receive adequate amounts of moisture without being subjected to heavy rains which would dislodge seedlings and even mature plants, leach essential minerals from their bodies and, in the case of tank bromeliads, wash impounded and accumulated nutrient material from leaf axils.

A few bromeliads inhabit nearly rainless coastal deserts; others survive

3

temporary but frequent submersion by flooding water courses; still others grow so close to the ocean that they are regularly subjected to salt sprays which would kill most other plants. Numerous species of all three subfamilies live in open terrain, as saxicole on rocks and canyon cliffs, or epiphytically on the uppermost branches of trees where they are exposed throughout the year to the full force of the sun.

But not all environmental barriers have been breached with equal success; no bromeliad can tolerate prolonged sub-zero temperatures, although some species have adapted to high tropical mountains where nights can be frosty. In Peru, for example, some tillandsias still occur at 4000 m altitude; *Puya raimondii*, which at flowering reaches a height of 39 ft (12 m) and is the largest bromeliad, grows between 4000 and 4300 m in the Peruvian Andes, and *Puya nivalis* in Colombia even approaches the snow line at 4800 m.

Bromeliads rarely achieve dominant status in any of the various habitats in which they are represented. Notable exceptions are *Tillandsia paleacea*, *T. straminea*, *T. purpurea* and *T. latifolia* which grow in almost pure stands in the Peruvian coastal deserts. Rain is exceedingly rare in this region and the only reliable moisture available is provided by fog, locally known as 'garua', which drifts in from the Pacific and may enshroud the coastal land for months. Here these tillandsias cover the desert sand in often enormous numbers to the exclusion of most other higher plants. But dominance is achieved here by default since there are essentially no other plant competitors capable of enduring with equal success such hostile conditions.

In less severe habitats, and particularly in forest communities, bromeliads usually constitute only a minor component of the total plant biomass. But they nevertheless often play a very significant and even essential role in the life of the forest. In many localities the water-holding tanks formed by the leaf rosettes of many bromeliads represent the only source of fresh water for many animals during the long dry season or periods of drought. Insects with aquatic larval stages heavily depend on the presence of tank bromeliads, and a number of species of tree frogs breed exclusively in the small pools of water provided by these plants. Small reptiles, amphibians and many invertebrates seek out the shelter between bromeliad leaves in order to keep moist and cool. Several species of aquatic carnivorous bladderworts have become so highly selective in their growing requirements that their occurrence is essentially restricted to the water-holding tanks of certain bromeliads. In general, the bromeliad tank supports an often diverse and complex plant and animal community and in return derives valuable nutrients from its wastes and break-down products.

An interesting variation to the theme of nutrient procurement and interaction of different life forms is encountered in many 'bulb' producing tillandsias such as *Tillandsia caput-medusae*, *T. seleriana*, *T. butzii*

4

and others, where cavities within the 'bulb' are formed by consecutive layers of inflated leaf bases which are constricted at the top, thus allowing little access from the exterior. These cavities are frequently inhabited by colonies of ants which can serve the plant in two ways: by protecting it against plant-eating predators and by providing nutritional supplements from their excreta.

CHAPTER 2

INTRODUCTION TO
HORTICULTURE

Bromeliads first became important in horticulture during the nineteenth century, but their introduction to the Western world started over 300 years earlier, with Christopher Columbus' second voyage to the New World in 1493. During this voyage the explorer discovered the pineapple being cultivated by the Indian population on the islands of Guadeloupe in the West Indies. Columbus brought the plant back to Spain and introduced it to the Spanish Court where it soon became very popular. From here it rapidly spread throughout the more tropical parts of the world during the early 1500s.

The cultivation of pineapples in Europe did not really commence until the seventeenth century when heated glasshouses began to be built for the successful propagation of tender plants. However, these structures were expensive and only the very rich and the aristocracy could afford them. Some other bromeliads were now being introduced and when Linnaeus in 1753 published his *Species Plantarum* he listed 14 plants of the bromeliad family. At this time these 14 were listed under two genera—*Bromelia* (for the plants with spines) and *Tillandsia* (for those with spineless leaves). Other botanists rapidly subdivided these two genera and introduced new names such as *Pitcairnea* and *Ananas*. The family Bromeliaceae was established by the French botanist Auguste Jaume de Saint-Hilaire in the late eighteenth century.

During the later part of the eighteenth century and the early part of the nineteenth century there was a marked upsurge in interest in obtaining and cultivating exotic plants. This was the time of establishment of many of the large firms who sent out collectors to all parts of the globe to discover and send home new plants.

Some of the first bromeliads introduced (after the pineapple) were *Bromelia pinguin*, *Guzmania lingulata*, *Bromelia humilis*, *Bromelia chrysantha* and *Bromelia karatas*. These were followed (in the early nineteenth century) by *Billbergia pyramidalis*, *Billbergia zebrina*, *Aechmea fasciata*, *Aechmea pectinata*, *Cryptanthus bromelioides* and *Vriesea splendens*.

Much of the interest in bromeliads in the nineteenth century centred in France and Belgium. Many new plants were introduced and first described in the French and Belgian publications *Revue Horticole*, *La Belgique Horticole* and *L'Illustration Horticole*. Many others were illustrated and described in *Curtis' Botanical Magazine*, *The Botanical Cabinet* and *The Botanical Register*.

Amongst the collectors of this period were Linden, Roezl Wallis and Giesbrecht whose names have been recorded within the species names of plants they collected. They collected many other kinds of plants as well as bromeliads, particularly orchids, begonias and gesneriads.

The largest collections at this time were in Belgium, such as that of Makoy in Liege. The leading authority on the family was also Belgian, Professor Charles Morren. Two of Morren's students were André and Mez, both of whom became authorities on the family following Morren's death.

André made a major collecting expedition to Colombia and Ecuador in 1875–6 and on his return published a monograph called *Bromeliaceae Andreanae* in which he described and illustrated 122 species and 14 varieties of which 91 were new. This beautiful publication is still of interest to the serious bromeliad fancier and has recently been republished.

The other student of Morren's, Carl Mez, in 1935 published in Engler's *Das Pflanzenreich* (The Plant Kingdom) the most complete monograph on the family up to that time. It remained the authoritative work on bromeliads for the next 40 years.

At approximately the same time as André was introducing bromeliads into Europe a Frenchman, August Glaziou, was collecting and introducing bromeliads into the horticulture of their native country, Brazil. As a professional horticulturist to the Emperor of Brazil he was particularly well placed to carry out this task. Bromeliads were only a small part of the floral wealth of Brazil that was available to Glaziou, but he introduced 65 species which is a number exceeded only by a very few other collectors.

Towards the end of the nineteenth century there were many other European collectors working in South America and they also introduced quite a number of new bromeliads. Many of their names have been incorporated into the botanical names of these plants.

Also at this time some European growers began experimenting with the production of new types of bromeliads through hybridisation. Many genera were used but *Billbergia* and *Vriesea* were the most popular; in the case of the former probably because of the spectacular flowers and bracts (even if short-lived) and the ease of raising the hybrids. In the case of the latter, it was the long-lasting and spectacular inflorescence which was most appreciated and the work of hybridisation has continued through many generations right up to the present day. Certain hybrids have also been line bred through many generations of continual selection and now produce magnificent plants with relatively fixed characteristics.

The interest in new introductions and hybrids continued until the outbreak of World War I, which put a sudden stop to these horticultural activities. Many of the large collections on the continent were lost over this period and the interval between World Wars I and II saw little revival in interest except in isolated instances. After World War II, except for Professor Rauh at the University of Heidelberg and Walter Richter in East Germany, the main interest in bromeliads returned to the USA. However, the largest private collection in the world has been that of Julien Marnier-Lapostolle at Cap-Ferrat on the Mediterranean coast of southern France.

The person responsible for collecting and introducing more bromeliads than anyone else is Mulford Foster of Orlando, Florida. In 1935 he and his wife, Racine Foster, made a number of trips to South America to find and introduce new plants. During the course of these expeditions, which are excitingly described in his book *Brazil, Orchid of the Tropics*, Foster brought back over 200 bromeliads that were new to horticulture. As well, he made many hybrids at a time when there was almost no activity in these plants anywhere else in the world.

His enthusiasm and all the new material was primarily responsible for the formation in 1950 of The Bromeliad Society as an international organisation devoted to enlarging and extending interest in these plants.

Following this, many other collectors from the USA and Europe continued to explore and collect in Central and South America. At the present time we are also seeing an upsurge in interest by the local botanists and horticulturists in the Americas, mainly directed towards identification and conservation of species before destruction of the habitat of many of these plants occurs.

The Introduction of Bromeliads into the United Kingdom

No precise records exist as to how bromeliads found their way into the realm of popularity in Britain. There is a splendid picture hanging in the Victoria and Albert Museum in London which depicts a presentation of the first pineapple grown in England to King Charles II by his gardener. This would seem to indicate the authenticity of the record that *Ananas*, at least, had been introduced during the mid- to late 1600s.

From this time information is rather vague, and in a sense came to a halt. It was not until the mid-eighteenth century that *Pitcairnia* receives reference, and the very few species known in that day appear to have been of West Indian origin.

It is therefore very certain that bromeliads began to make an in-road into Britain early in the nineteenth century when species of *Aechmea*, *Billbergia*, *Cryptanthus*, *Nidularium* and *Guzmania* became fashionable within a limited sphere of the more 'privileged' who were able to provide stove-house facilities to accomodate such exotics. Later that century saw the introduction of other genera, and the interest increased as a better understanding of these plants became apparent. There is evidence that plants of *Dyckia*, *Hechtia* and other terrestrials had attracted the attention of fanciers, not to mention the epiphytic *Canistrum* from Brazil. In just a few years *Fascicularia* captured the imagination of enthusiastic plant-lovers, due in no small degree to the hardiness of certain species in southerly parts of Britain. It is also known that Kew Gardens recorded about 100 different bromeliad species in 1864.

Interest gained headway just prior to, and certainly following, World War I. Expeditions were carefully planned which resulted in more species being introduced. Even then they were not easily acquired by the ordinary individual and remained the pleasure of the privileged few. This period saw the entry of different species of *Vriesea* and only a handful of *Tillandsia* such as *T. cyanea* and *T. lindenii*, which were cultivated as pot plants.

However, from about 1946, commercial growers became involved in the propagation of bromeliads, and possibly outstanding amongst these was the Thomas Rochford organisation headed by Tom Rochford himself, a plantsman of great merit. Such enterprises made these remarkable plants available to the public. They quickly became coveted for home décor; with the upsurge of the building of—and heating of—greenhouses by numerous British gardeners, they were also quickly established as suitable subjects for culture. Today, there are a number of establishments specialising in the propagation of various bromeliad species and cultivars. The 'air-plant' vogue came to the fore about 1979–80 when various *Tillandsia* species were offered to the general public affixed to pieces of cork, driftwood, rock or crystal. The credit for this type of presentation is undoubtedly due to the initiative of the late Victoria Padilla who for many years, indeed from its conception, was the Editor of the Bromeliad Society Journal of America. Where previously these dwarf plants had been carefully wired or tied to bunches of twigs or pieces of wood, she conceived the idea of gluing them in place. This procedure was followed in Britain, so that today close on 200 different tillandsias can be obtained and grown successfully in this way.

Mention must also be made of one of the most outstanding collections in Britain which has been assembled by Mr. L. Maurice Mason of Fincham in Norfolk. His enthusiasm took him on extensive explorations in search of plants, especially in Costa Rica and other Central American countries. Today, a vast glasshouse is devoted entirely to bromeliads—

numerous species including the less common *Wittrockia*, *Fernseea* and the like. Another ardent enthusiast—and authority—Peter Temple has maintained one of the most worth-while collections in Britain. His knowledge made it possible for him to carry through so successfully the translation into English of Werner Rauh's *Bromelien* which has subsequently become one of the foremost presentations on bromeliads for the English-speaking world.

In 1967 there were a great number of collectors of cacti and succulent plants who had gradually gathered certain bromeliad species into their collections. A number, such as *Dyckia*, *Hechtia*, *Bromelia* and *Puya*, had become accepted as 'succulents'—and when epiphytic succulents gained considerable popularity during the earlier 1960s, many included *Tilland-sia* species in their interest. All this probably led up to the formation of the British Bromeliad Society in 1968, following endless correspondence and discussions between Clive Innes, who had well over 1200 different species occupying one of his greenhouses in Ashington, West Sussex, and an ardent epiphytic enthusiast, A.J.S. McMillan of Bristol. These two, with the help of Bill Wall, Peter Temple, Ron Lucibell and others decided to launch the Society—and in a comparatively short space of time a numerically strong organisation had become established, this momentum continually gaining favour with a well-received *Journal* being published in September 1968 and edited by A.J.S. McMillan. A number of shows were arranged, and to no small degree the success of these must be laid to the efforts of Ron Lucibell whose skill in organisation won much approval. But the increasing difficulty of finding a suitable meeting place or places, led to the meetings being discontinued. To a great measure the Society maintained its identity due to Ron Lucibell, who had taken over the production as well as the editing of the *Journal*. This continued regularly until early 1987 when Ron found it necessary to 'call it a day'. Hopes of its revival are now very encouraging due to the initiative of Stuart Houghton, in conjunction with Barbara Dobbins from the USA and now domiciled in Britain (see Appendix 1). Encouragement has been given by Stapeley Water Gardens of Nantwich, Cheshire who have offered space to create a National Collection of Bromeliads, and this offer has been enthusiastically welcomed. The work is in progress, gaining support from many directions, not only from Stuart who is the prime mover in this project, but also from John Emery of Vesutor Air Plants of Billingshurst in West Sussex, and others.

There are a number of excellent collections of bromeliads within the UK. Kew Gardens have built up a remarkably extensive display including many of the more uncommon species of *Tillandsia*, *Vriesea*, *Guzmania* and *Aechmea*. These are attractively featured as growing epiphytically on improvised tree-trunks. The terrestrial species of *Pitcairnia*, *Ananas*, *Cryptanthus*, *Dyckia* and others are most effectively arranged.

The Royal Horticultural Society's Garden at Wisley have mustered a fine collection amongst their collection of exotics—as has the Edinburgh Botanic Garden in Scotland.

Hybridisation of bromeliads has not been undertaken to any great degree in the UK—such plants, and there are a great number of them, have primarily found their way to Britain from Holland, Belgium and, to a lesser extent, from the USA. The general attitude has been 'let us thoroughly explore the potential of the species before indulging too much in hybrids'—worthy though they be.

Conservation of Bromeliads

In common with other groups of ornamental houseplants, such as orchids, cacti and other succulents, wild populations of bromeliads are beginning to face the threat of extinction as consumer demands for these attractive plants continue to increase. The Bromeliaceae is a large family containing over 2000 species in about 46 genera, and of these only about 1 per cent are commonly cultivated while a further 9 per cent are commercially available through specialist dealers but more rarely grown.

Not surprisingly and as with other large plant families the Bromeliaceae has common, often weedy species that have become very successful through adaptation. Among these is the Spanish moss, *Tillandsia usneoides*. This species is very common throughout its range and is frequently seen growing on telegraph wires and from other suitable anchorage points in the southern USA and neighbouring Mexico. It is often used as a desiccant in packing and is considered a serious nuisance in some areas. Also very widely grown and selectively bred through domestication is the pineapple, *Ananas comosus*, probably the only member of the family readily recognised as internationally commercially important. At the other extreme many species are considered to be on the verge of extinction either because of their beauty and hence desirability from gardening enthusiasts or else as a result of habitat destruction, which now poses a serious threat to many of these plants, that are entirely New World in origin (with the exception of one species of *Pitcairnea* from West Africa).

Of all the genera, *Tillandsia* with some 400 species, is probably the most important. As already mentioned, many of the species are sold as 'air-plants' and are often anchored on to shells, corals, tree fern bark or gnarled bogwood for resale by the major chainstores and plant centres. This genus contains some of the rarest and most sought after species in the family and according to Professor Werner Rauh, one of the leading authorities on bromeliads, those considered most threatened include the Mexican *T. argentea*, *T. atroviridipetala*, *T. butzii*, *T. caput-medusae*, *T. filifolia*, *T. ignesiana*, *T. ionantha*, *T. magnusiana*, *T. mauryana*,

T. plumosa, *T. pruinosa* and *T. streptophylla*. Also seriously threatened are *T. tectorum* and *T. cacticola* from Peru, *T. xerographica* from Guatemala and all the small species from the Organ Mountains in Brazil.

Although all the grey-leaved tillandsias can be grown from seed they may take several years to reach maturity and stripping plants from the wild is, at least in the short term, a more financially viable proposition. Because of this, several international conservation organisations have voiced their concern for these plants.

The UK-based Fauna and Flora Preservation Society (FFPS) commissioned Mike Read, an independent environmental consultant, to investigate the extent of trade in bromeliads in 1987. He reported back at a meeting held in Ottawa, Canada later that year. At the same time another international organisation—Trade Records Analysis of Flora and Fauna in Commerce, usually known by their acronym TRAFFIC, commissioned a similar study in West Germany. This report was presented at the Plants Committee meeting of the Convention on International Trade in Endangered Species of wild fauna and flora (CITES) held at the Royal Botanic Gardens, Kew in 1988. Their results showed that between 50 and 70 per cent of plants entering international trade were still coming from the wild. Between January 1987 and March 1988, 137 tonnes of bromeliads were exported from Guatemala to ten European and North American countries with West Germany taking 54 per cent, the USA 12 per cent and the UK 4 per cent.

Although mature plants are grown-on in the Guatemalan nurseries until their offsets are large enough to be removed, they are not maintained as stock plants. This means that regular forays into the forests to collect more plants are the usual means of keeping stock plants replenished. It was also found that trees were felled solely to fill this requirement. Seed propagation is not normally practised. On the positive side, one West German nurseryman working closely with the Guatemalans is researching propagation techniques to speed the development of seed-raised or vegetatively propagated plants and hopefully will be able to introduce these methods into Guatemala in the near future.

Both of the reports mentioned above recommended CITES listing for bromeliads. Three Appendices list the species protected by CITES and Appendix II is the most widely used. This means that trade in any species or group listed is monitored by an internationally recognised licence system. Appendix I listing effectively bans trade and contains only those species thought to be seriously threatened by international trade. For example, ten orchids out of 25,000 occur on this list. Appendix III helps countries to enforce existing legislation protecting their native species and could be used by Guatemala if they so choose. Sadly, Mexico, home of many of the rarest species, is not a party to the convention.

Although most conservationists would like to see blanket protection for bromeliads this is probably not a practical solution under the present system. If all 2000 species were listed on Appendix II, many of the very common species would be subject to licensing and for obvious reasons time would be wasted unnecessarily, while the rarer species were pushed closer to extinction. Perhaps specific listing of the most endangered species on Appendix I would be the best approach. Dialogue between all the different agencies involved is the best way forward in developing a strategy for the future.

CHAPTER 3

THE BROMELIAD FAMILY

The bromeliad family consists of approximately 2000 known species with more being discovered. These highly desirable plants can be found from the southern United States to as far south as Argentina. To discuss them generally in this book would be ineffective unless we can recognise the various groupings used by the collector and horticulturist to identify and describe the numerous plants available.

Bromeliads can be broken down to three subfamilies, namely Pitcairnioideae, Tillandsioideae and Bromelioideae, and then different genera within these subfamilies.

Pitcairnioideae

Pitcairnioideae has 13 genera, which in turn subdivide into about 700 species.

Abromeitiella

Consists of two species, found growing in dense mats on rocks in hot dry areas of Bolivia and Argentina. They appear to be miniature dyckias attaining rosettes of ⅕–1 in (2–2.5 cm) in diameter. Both plants have greenish-white flowers, and although not noteworthy are often grown as a curiosity because they are the only true cushion type in the subfamily. These plants are best grown in small containers.

Ayensua

One species exists which is deciduous and of little interest to horticulturists except as a curiosity.

Brocchinia

A little-known genus coming from the fabled 'lost world' of Venezuela and Guyana. They grow in one of the most isolated parts of the world, usually in large clumps in swampy areas or on exposed cliffs. About 18 species have so far been identified; all are large plants, attaining a height of

14

about 23 ft (7 m). They are known mainly by botanists and the one species growing in cultivation is *Brocchinia micrantha* from Venezuela.

Connellia
Found only in the isolated regions of Venezuela and Guyana known as the 'lost world' and not in general cultivation, three species are included in this genus. Terrestrial, it resembles a Puya.

Deuterocohnia
Approximately eight species discovered and few in cultivation, they are drought-resistant and found growing in adverse conditions on the rocky slopes of the Andean range. *Deuterocohnia meziana* is unique among bromeliads as its 6 ft (1.8 m) inflorescence continues to flower from the same scape for six to eight years.

Dyckia
Among terrestrial bromeliads dyckias are probably the best known; they are robust plants that require little care and attention. Heavily spined and growing under the same conditions as cacti and succulents, dyckias are small plants which make excellent subjects for the cool greenhouse.

There are about 100 known species. Some of the smaller forms such as *Dyckia fosteriana* and *Dyckia brevifolia* form large clumps very quickly and produce a profusion of colour at flowering. Most species have green leaves and vary in size from 4 in (10 cm) in diameter to the largest, *Dyckia maritima*, which flowers well above the height of the average person.

They have flower petals in a range of colours from orange to yellow and are carried on tall stalks emerging from the edge of the centre of the plant rather than the middle which is the case in other bromeliads. Dyckias are highly recommended to the beginner as a starting plant because of their ability to survive almost any conditions.

Encholirium
Approximately eight species discovered which resemble the genus *Dyckia* in appearance; rarely seen in cultivation.

Fosterella
Thirteen known species, all small terrestrial plants. They may be spined or smooth leaved and their branched inflorescence bears tiny white flowers. When in flower the plant is approximately 18 in (45 cm) high.

Hechtia
This group consists of about 40 species and ranges in size from several centimetres to about 3¼ ft (1 m) across.

As with most members of the subfamily Pitcairnioideae they too are heavily armed with marginal spines and require great care when handling. Hechtias are terrestrial and grow on desert hillsides and rocky slopes alongside cacti and are truly xerophytic, withstanding long periods of drought and extreme variations in temperature. The flowers of this genus are mainly insignificant and nearly always white in colour. Hence they are usually grown for their glossy foliage rather than their flowers.

Navia

Again a bromeliad from the 'lost world'. About 74 species make up the genus and these are mainly xerophytic. They grow on moist ledges as well as dry cliffs and vary greatly in size from very small to 2 ft (60 cm) in diameter. Two species, *Navia splendens* and *Navia arida*, have been grown successfully in cultivation. In habitat they are terrestrial or saxicolous and often form large clumps. The inflorescence is sessile in the centre of the rosette, formed by the leaves which bear spines along the margins.

Pitcairnia

This genus has approximately 260 species and is one of the most striking plants, when in flower, in the Pitcairnioideae subfamily. Unlike the previous members of this subfamily, pitcairnia are found growing in moist, shady positions and some have been found growing epiphytically. Most of these plants are grass-like and for the most part smooth edged, lacking the spines generally found in other Pitcairnioideae genera. They bear tubular flowers with yellow, red or white petals and, although each flower lasts only a single day, the rather tall, thin inflorescence will continue to bloom for several months.

Within this group is the only bromeliad found growing outside the Americas, *Pitcairnia feliciana*. This species can be found growing on rocks and cliff faces in Guinea in Africa.

Puya

This genus, which contains about 168 species, is the oldest and most primitive of all bromeliads. Not only is it the oldest, but one species, *Puya raimondii* is the largest. This giant may reach 40 ft (12 m) in height and takes over 100 years to develop a flower spike. This is a truly remarkable bromeliad as its inflorescence consists of masses of flowers arranged on a stem approximately 2–3 ft (60–90 cm) in diameter and containing about 30,000 individual flowers.

All puyas are terrestrial or saxicolous, existing in areas of extreme climatic conditions, from snow to deserts. They range in height from 1 ft (30 cm) to 33 ft (10 m) and all have stiff, spiny leaves with cruel barbs along the edges. As a rule they grow in large clumps and therefore are not for the average collector. They are usually best grown in botanical gardens where space is not a problem. Flowers in this group are tubular and consist of three main colours, green, lavender and blue; however there are some with white flowers, and their size ranges from ⅕–4 in (2–10 cm) in length.

Tillandsioideae

Tillandsioieae is the second subfamily, consisting of about 50 per cent of the known bromeliads. Six genera make up this subfamily.

Catopsis
These plants are epiphytes and comprise about 26 known species. They are soft leaved, smooth edged, and form graceful small rosettes. The undersides of the leaves are coated with what appears to be white powder. The flowers have white or yellow petals and are very small. The catopsis are interesting plants but not highly decorative.

Glomeropitcairnia
Only two species are known to exist—*Glomeropitcairnia penduliflora* and *Glomeropitcairnia erectiflora*. As with all plants in the subfamily they are spineless. Both plants take many years to bloom and are rarely found in cultivation.

Guzmania
There are today approximately 150 species that have been identified and described. They are in the main epiphytes growing on trees, but a few larger specimens are terrestrial. Most guzmanias are found in moist shaded forests that are very humid. The inflorescence usually extends above the rosette formed by the leaves and displays brilliant coloration for long periods. The flower bracts are yellow to orange or red and the flowers usually have white or red petals. This is a genus that requires some warmth during the winter months to be at its best.

Mezobromelia
A rare genus which is not found in cultivation and only two species have been identified. They are similar to guzmania, epiphytic and grow at high altitudes. The two known species are *Mezobromelia bicolor* and *Mezobromelia fulgens*.

Tillandsia
This genus has the largest number of species and the greatest natural distribution, from southern United States to southern Argentina. Tillandsias are a variable species that range in size from the tiniest of plants, *Tillandsia bryoides*, approximately ⅓ in (1 cm) to *Tillandsia grandis* with

its inflorescence towering up to 10 ft (3 m). *Tillandsia usneoides*, Spanish Moss, can be seen growing in long wispy strands from large oaks in the southern states of America and few movies made in these areas fail to show it in some background scene. About 500 Tillandsia species have been identified and more will follow, as tillandsias are the bromeliad collector's dream. Most are very hardy in cultivation and reward the grower with long-lasting, exquisite blooms.

The higher altitude tillandsias are extremely difficult to grow and should be avoided by novice collectors. Tillandsias are mainly tree dwellers, with some larger specimens being terrestrial. They use their roots as hold-fasts, attaching themselves to their host with wire-like roots that have little if any use in the nourishment of the plant. Some, like *Tillandsia duratii* var. *saxatilis*, never show any sign of root growth, but will multiply and flower regularly. Tillandsias are true 'air-plants' existing only on moisture and nutrients that can be obtained from the air. Good air movement is required to grow these plants well as they are generally found in exposed areas.

Generally the flowers are tubular and violet-blue in colour, although some have white, pink or yellow flowers. The floral bracts vary from lifeless grey to red and some species are highly scented, particularly at night. There are a large number of tillandsias in cultivation and they are very much sought after by beginners and enthusiasts.

Vriesea

These have been favourites in Europe since the 1830s and for good reasons. About 250 species have been described and all are worth collecting. They are very adaptable to cultivation, which makes them exceptional houseplants. Vrieseas are found in rainforests and are primarily epiphytes, growing in partial shade with good air circulation and high humidity. Generally they are medium-sized plants, with smooth, spineless leaves and produce flattened inflorescences resembling a sword, usually with yellow flowers. Flowering takes many months and inflorescences are nearly always upright, reaching a height of 9 ft (2.7 m) and containing some hundreds of individual flowers in *Vriesea imperialis*, one of the largest of the genus. *Vriesea imperialis* is terrestrial and grows to approximately 5 ft (1.5 m) in diameter.

Vrieseas, because of their wide range of habitat, are tolerant of cold temperatures and are ideal plants for the beginner to start with when acquiring a collection. There is wide variation in their foliage, texture and markings. Some have firm, glossy leaves, others are marked with cross-banding of remarkable beauty and some, like *Vriesea guttata*, are speckled. Others resemble tillandsias, such as *Vriesea incurva* and *Vriesea espinosae*, which have tillandsia-like leaves and grey scales.

All in all, vrieseas are worth collecting no matter which species.

Bromelioideae

Bromelioideae is the third subfamily of these remarkable plants and it consists of 27 genera, containing hundreds of species.

Acanthostachys

The only species in this genus, *Acanthostachys strobilacea*, is unique in the bromeliad world because of the way it cascades on long, thin, terete, spiny leaves, which emerge from a stoloniferous caudex. The long-lasting inflorescence resembles a miniature pineapple approximately 1 in (2.5 cm) long and ⅓ in (1 cm) in diameter. This species is found growing as an epiphyte in tropical rainforests.

Aechmea

Aechmeas lend themselves to cultivation more readily than any other bromeliad and therefore are more widely grown and thereby more available. Several hundred species have been identified and probably the best known would be *Aechmea fasciata*, which was introduced into cultivation in 1826. Aechmeas are saxicolous, terrestrial and epiphytic. The beauty of their foliage, and their long-lasting inflorescence, are contributing factors to their popularity. Adaptability to house conditions, pot culture and their general overall hardiness, add to their appeal.

The varieties available are almost infinite and their shape, size and colour is extremely variable, from a few centimetres to about 10 ft (3 m) in diameter (*Aechmea conifera*). There is a plant for everyone. The leaves of this genus may be plain green, maroon, rose, brown; striated and extremely rigid or delicately soft. They may be spread out in open rosettes or tubular in form. The inflorescence usually rises above the plant on a sizeable scape, with very colourful bracts. The inflorescence after flowering holds berry-like fruit, which is a distinguishing 'trademark' of the *Aechmea* genus. They grow in exposed conditions or full shade, on windswept mountains or forest floors. All do well in cultivation and very few require any special attention.

Ananas

This genus includes the commercial pineapple, *Ananas comosus* and several variegated forms, namely *Ananas comosus* var. *variegatus*. Most people have eaten the fruit of pineapples but very few have known that they are part of the bromeliad family. The genus consists of eight species and all have extremely spiny margins, usually with hooked spines. The inflorescence rises from the centre of the plant and forms a fruiting head, which can be cut off and planted to form new suckers. All ananas have flowers with purple-blue petals.

19

Andrea

The only species is *Andrea selloana* which is native to southern Brazil. According to available information it is not currently grown in cultivation.

Androlepis

The only species, *Androlepis skinneri*, grows on rocks or epiphytically in forests. The inflorescence is branched and slightly arched, the bracts are pale and the flowers have bright yellow petals.

Araeococcus

There are four known species, of which only two are in cultivation, *Araeococcus flagellifolius* and *Araeococcus pectinatus*. Both grow as epiphytes and are not commonly available.

Billbergia

About 54 species make up the genus. They are colourful and easily grown. *Billbergia nutans* and *Billbergia pyramidalis* are among the most easily grown species. Billbergias are easily identified from most other bromeliads as they generally have fewer leaves and are tall and tubular in appearance. Foliage can be mottled, crossbanded or variegated. Their inflorescences, although lasting from only a few days to possibly two weeks, are perhaps the most beautiful of all bromeliads. They have tubular flowers, with recurved petals in a variety of striking colours, usually purple, blue, yellow, green or white and most inflorescences are of a cascading nature. Billbergias will tolerate almost all conditions in cultivation but should be given strong light and hard conditions.

Bromelia

Consists of around 50 species which could not be classified as 'delicate'. They are large, robust plants with barbed leaves and often form impenetrable barriers. In parts of South America they are grown as hedges to fence in cattle. Extremely large plants, they may reach a diameter of 6 ft (1.8 m) at maturity. When not flowering they resemble a pineapple. They are terrestrial in habitat and some species, *Bromelia balansae* for example, are very colourful at maturity. A few of the species have some economic value as their fruit is used in medications.

Canistrum

This genus consists of seven species which are large plants reaching 2–3 ft (60–90 cm) in diameter. They prefer moist conditions and grow either as terrestrials or epiphytes. The inflorescence is deep in the heart of the rosette and the compact flower head is surrounded by colourful bracts rising above the flowers, creating an effect like a basket of flowers.

The foliage is predominantly light green with darker green mottling. Easy to grow and worthy of collection.

Cryptanthus

Forty-eight species belong to this genus and are commonly called 'earth stars' because of the flattish form and symmetry of their leaves. They are terrestrials and grow under a wide range of conditions; from full sun to total shade, dry to wet, and in open landscape or on forest floors. They are small plants ranging from about 2–18 in (5–45 cm) in diameter and almost all grow as low, spreading, stemless rosettes. Cryptanthus come in various colours: rose, silver, green, brown, white, copper or combinations of these. All have white flowers deep in the heart of the plant. Offsets are produced by stolons or from the edge of the rosette. They are easy to grow and flourish well in cultivation. Because of their size, some are used regularly in floral arrangements. A must for any collector.

Fascicularia

This genus contains five species, which grow naturally in Chile, South America. Extremely hardy, they like full sunlight and can withstand cool nights. In their natural habitat they grow in exposed areas near the sea, in soil or on rock cliff faces. At flowering time the leaves turn red at the centre of the plant. Two species are found in cultivation, namely *Fascicularia bicolor* and *Fascicularia pitcairnifolia*.

Fernseea

Only one species exists, *Fernseea itatiaiae*. This is a small xerophytic plant, with firm, narrow, heavily spined leaves 6–7 in (15–18 cm) long. It is not known to be in cultivation.

Greigia

About 20 species of these large terrestrial plants have been identified. Greigias are rare in cultivation as they grow in cool moist cloud forests at elevations of 2500 to 4000 m and are difficult to grow at low elevations. Unlike other bromeliads they do not die after flowering but continue to bloom every year from the same rosette.

Hohenbergia

Very few of the 36 species can be found in cultivation as they are too large and their inflorescences are colourless and uninteresting. *Hohenbergia stellata* is the exception with its brilliant red inflorescence which lasts for many months.

Neoglaziovia

Rare in cultivation, only two species are identified. A succulent-type leaf is the hallmark of these species, with inflorescences whose flowers are purple or violet. *Neoglaziovia variegata* has leaves which are green on the upper side and wide, white crossbanding on the underside. It is worth collecting when offered for sale.

Neoregelia

Around 71 species have been described, mainly natives of eastern Brazil. They are medium-sized, compact plants growing terrestrially or on lower limbs of trees in shaded areas. No bromeliad can offer a wider variety of leaf-texture or a selection of such colours. They are one of the most prized possessions in one's collection because of the large range of colours and sizes available. Neoregelias have been used extensively for hybridising and the results have produced some truly remarkable plants. They range in size from very small plants 5 in (12 cm) high and 1 in (2.5 cm) in diameter to plants 4 ft (1.2 m) in diameter (*Neoregelia carcharodon*).

The inflorescence forms a compound head nestled in the centre of the rosette and the flowers usually have blue or white petals. Neoregelias grow well in cultivation and reward the collector with a flush of colour at maturity that has to be seen to be believed. Well worth the effort in obtaining the best possible varieties available.

Nidularium

A small genus comprising 30 species, all native to eastern Brazil. Nidulariums are medium-sized plants with inflorescences forming low in the centre of the rosettes. At flowering time the collarette of shortened inner leaves turns brilliant red, rose or cerise, depending on the species. The flowers are red, white or blue and the leaves are usually glossy and finely spined.

In some varieties the inflorescence rises above the plant and creates a striking picture. *Nidularium seidelii* is such a plant, the inflorescence rising approximately 1 ft (30 cm) above the flattened foliage, with bracts forming large, yellow-green, boat-like shapes atop each other. The inflorescence can last several months. Nidulariums are hardy and reward growers with good formations and regular flowering.

Ochagavia

Four species are known to exist. Succulent-type plants with a clustering habit, growing on rocks or terrestrially. One species, *Ochagavia carnea*, may sometimes be found in cultivation. It is a small plant whose inflorescence, the size of a tennis ball, is covered with red bracts and borne on a short scape. The flowers are pink with yellow stamens that protrude beyond the petals. A plant worth collecting.

Orthophytum
Consists of around 18 species and is relatively unknown. Found growing as clusters on rock faces in warm sunlight in mountainous regions of Brazil. They are semi-succulent plants and all species have white flowers and green or copper coloured leaves with soft spines. Four plants are sometimes found in cultivation, namely *Orthophytum vagans*, *Orthophytum rubrum*, *Orthophytum saxicola* and *Orthophytum navioides*. *All require little attention, demanding only plenty of light.*

Portea
This genus consists of six species and some are outstanding in their beauty. They are terrestrials and grow in full sun in the coastal regions of Rio de Janeiro in Brazil. Robust plants with large spines and when in bloom may reach 4 ft (1.2 m) in height. Their inflorescences are generally regarded as one of the most decorative combining delicate colours of lavender and pink to form colourful displays which last for months on end.

Pseudoananas
This is a monotypic genus and its species, *Pseudoananas sagenarius*, is commonly called the false pineapple. It is very similar to the genus *Ananas* but is more robust and generally larger. The flattened, succulent inflorescence protrudes above the foliage about 1 ft (30 cm) and is 6–8 in (15–20 cm) long, bearing pink bracts and lavender flowers. The fruit is edible and quite tasty, but unlike the genus *Ananas*, is not grown commercially.

Quesnelia
Over 30 species have been identified with approximately a third in cultivation. Primarily terrestrials growing in the coastal swamps of eastern Brazil. The larger varieties, *Quesnelia arvensis* for example, have large, green rosettes with a floral head of brilliant pink or red. The smaller species are tubular in shape, resembling billbergias, and are found growing epiphytically or on rocks in the coastal mountains.

Ronnbergia
A small genus not usually grown, only two species, *Ronnbergia columbiana* and *Ronnbergia morreniana*, are rarely seen. A small to medium-sized plant with a stoloniferous habit, the inflorescence forms a simple spike with blue-petalled flowers.

Streptocalyx
So far only 14 species have been identified. Usually epiphytic, growing high on trees in hot, humid jungle areas. Medium to large plants closely

related to the genus *Aechmea*. One exceptional species, *Streptocalyx floribundis*, is the giant of the genus with leaves 8½ ft (2.5 m) long and an inflorescence, containing a myriad of flowers, 8½ ft (2.5 m) in height. They require warm, humid conditions that can only be achieved in a greenhouse.

Wittrockia

Growing in the southern coastal mountains of Brazil, six species have so far been discovered and only two are seen in cultivation, *Wittrockia smithii* and *Wittrockia superba*. Epiphytic or terrestrial plants growing often in full sun or in medium intensity light about half-way up trees. Most species have thin leaves with few marginal spines; *Wittrockia superba* is the exception. The inflorescence is similar to that of the genus *Neoregelia* in most species.

As can be seen, the diversity of size, shape and colour of the bromeliad family, together with its remarkable biology, makes its members unique, interesting and highly desirable.

CHAPTER 4

How to Grow Bromeliads

Being of tropical or subtropical origin almost all bromeliads require protected, frost-free conditions if they are to be successfully grown in Britain. This means either growing them in heated greenhouses, conservatories or indoors as houseplants. Although bromeliads are of easy culture, each situation has both advantages and disadvantages which will help determine the range and type of plants that you can grow.

Due to the marked climatic differences over their distribution, the light and temperature requirements of bromeliads are not all the same. Some are inhabitants of lowland tropical rainforests while others come from cooler, drier regions found at higher altitudes. Large groups such as the tillandsias have species growing in all these many varied habitats which has resulted in the appearance of many different forms. At the cooler extreme are the familiar 'air-plants' that we see for sale in many garden centres and florists shops, which require high light conditions and can tolerate temperatures down as low as 50°F (10°C) or even lower if kept dry in winter.

By sustaining a minimum temperature of about 60°F (15°C), you will be able to grow all the bromeliad species and hybrids.

A temperature of 50°F (10°C) will preclude the tropical soft-leaved types such as many species of *Vriesia* and *Guzmania* while temperatures as low as 40°F (5°C) will reduce the selection to the stiff, succulent or grey-leaved types such as some species of tillandsia, puya and billbergia.

Light is important to the wellbeing of all bromeliads, although some require far more than others. Ground dwellers such as puya, dykia, and hechtia and hard or grey-leaved epiphytes such as tillandsia, aechmea and billbergia can be given full exposure to sunlight. This will encourage strong growth, good leaf coloration and patterning.

Other bromeliads such as neoregelia and guzmania require a little more shade, while the tropical soft-leaved types such as many aechmea, vriesia, nidularium and cryptanthus require semi-shaded positions. If the latter group are given too much strong sunlight, the leaves are prone to bleach or scorch, disfiguring the appearance of the plants.

25

Light exposure can be controlled by carefully positioning plants, placing those which require more light closer to the glass, keeping light sensitive species in the shade of others or by shading their location with special paints or fabrics.

Greenhouses

For many, a greenhouse is the obvious place in which to grow bromeliads. Those with houses can alter or adapt their existing growing conditions to suit or just grow those species which are best adapted. For example, succulent enthusiasts may not be able to grow the tropical soft-leaved kinds but will be able to grow those from more arid habitats such as dyckia, hechtia, and many grey-leaved tillandsias. Orchid enthusiasts on the other hand will be able to accommodate those from more tropical regions.

For those new to greenhouse growing, site is all important as this determines the light conditions and to some degree the ambient temperature of the house.

Ideally it should face south, so that the maximum amount of light can enter the house, particularly in winter when the sun angle is low. Avoid north, as this provides the poorest light although it will be acceptable for tropical species as long as you can maintain the temperatures. At all costs, try not to place your greenhouse in the permanent shade of buildings or trees. You can always reduce the light intensity quite cheaply, but it is more difficult and expensive to increase it.

A rectangular house should have its ridge orientated east-west to obtain the best light. There are many houses available today either octagonal or hexagonal in shape which make very acceptable and attractive homes for bromeliads.

The best greenhouse frameworks are made either in timber or aluminium. On the whole timber houses are more expensive than aluminium types and can entail more general maintenance. However, they are attractive to look at and are marginally warmer in winter. Aluminium frameworks are lighter, narrower and cheaper than wood. They also allow in more light but can have a harsh appearance. Some manufacturers are now making them with coloured components.

The size of the house will obviously dictate the size and number of plants you can grow. In smaller houses, the number of large rosette plants will have to be reduced. The miniature species of cryptanthus, dyckia and tillandsia will obviously make a better choice. Epiphytic kinds can be fastened to cork bark sections and hung from the roof, thus utilising space that is normally wasted in many greenhouses.

Heating

Heating greenhouses is really down to making a choice over the cost of maintaining the desired minimum temperature and the size of the house.

No matter what form of heating you choose select a model which will easily maintain your minimum temperature, not just struggle as soon as the weather turns bad. Just one night of very cold weather could see off much of your collection if the heating cannot cope.

The choice of heating appliances is wide and varied. Those who require permanent installations could choose an oil-fired boiler with heating pipes running around the bottom of the walls. They are expensive but effective and reliable.

An electricity supply is an important asset for any greenhouse. It not only allows you to install lighting, it also allows you to use electric heaters. These are probably the most popular and cheapest form of heating, particularly if your heater has thermostatic control so that it only comes on when required. Convector heaters will also blow warm air around the house, ensuring that it is properly distributed. The fans on some models can be used to blow cool air around the house in summer.

Those without electricity can either use paraffin or calor-gas heaters. Paraffin has, for many years, been the traditional method of heating. Many sizes are available but ensure that it is a 'blue flame' type which burns fuel evenly and does not produce fumes which may affect some plants. Extension arms are available for larger models which give a better distribution of heat. Calor gas and paraffin heaters both produce water vapour from burning fuel, which will tend to raise the humidity in winter.

Heating costs can be reduced by ensuring all possible leaks in the greenhouse framework are repaired. Refit slipped or broken glass, place a seal around a badly fitting door or ventilator. Double glazing kits are also available for greenhouses. The simplest is just a sheet of polythene but the modern 'bubble plastic' sheeting is more effective. It is made from laminated polythene in which bubbles of air have been trapped. Sheets come in pane widths. In timber houses it can be held with large drawing pins, in aluminium houses the sheets are held in place by clips which fit into the central groove of the glazing bar. Ensure that all the sheets overlap and there are no gaps. Sheets should be pulled as tight as possible to keep the layer of air trapped as effectively as possible. Cover the vents separately so that they can be opened if necessary.

Solid sheets of clear PVC can also be fixed to glazing bars as a more durable form of insulation.'

No matter which type you use, winter sunlight will be further reduced, particularly if it becomes dirty. Part or all of the insulation can be removed once danger of frost is past, if required.

Shading

Sun sensitive species will require shading from the effects of direct sunlight, particularly in summer. This can be achieved in a number of ways.

Shading can either be produced by using fabrics or paints. White, water-soluble, shading paints are applied to the outside of the glass. The amount applied will determine the amount of light reflected. A light stipple will provide a small amount while one or two heavy coats will provide shading suitable for soft-leaved tropical species.

One modern development is 'Verishade', a paint that becomes transparent during wet weather and opaque when sunny. Shading paints should be washed off with water in autumn.

Fabrics are also a popular method of providing shading. Open-mesh fabric woven from polypropylene thread is both light and durable. It can be hung from the inside using clips or pins as with insulation materials or it can be hung over the whole greenhouse. It can also be fixed as a roll along the top of the ridge and pulled down when required. Roller blinds are available for both greenhouses and conservatories, which although expensive to buy, are attractive to look at and convenient to use.

Light sensitive species can also be placed in the shade of other plants. They may also be placed beneath galvanised mesh or slatted timber staging.

Conservatories

A modern development, conservatories make ideal locations in which to show off bromeliads at their best. However, the growing environment of the conservatory is far different to that of the greenhouse.

Whereas the greenhouse is specifically designed for growing plants, the conservatory is foremost an extension of living space although plants do form an important part of the décor. Again if a choice is available, conservatories are usually situated on a south-facing wall where light conditions are best. There is not always freedom of choice and they may have to be situated on the only wall available. North is the worst for light conditions particularly as the structure will be permanently over-shadowed by the house. A solid roof will reduce light conditions still further.

Conservatories tend to be much larger than greenhouses, so larger specimen-sized plants can be grown. Greater volumes of space allow bromeliads to be displayed in semi-natural settings, such as being planted on sections of tree branches or on a model tree formed from strips of cork bark.

With some being tolerant of far more dry air than many other plants,

Figure 1   A collection of bromeliads in a conservatory, showing the spectacular range of forms.

bromeliads are a logical choice where the air has to be kept drier for reasons of comfort and to avoid damaging furnishings. Both user and plant will also benefit from being shaded in summer!

Indoors and Windowsills

Many bromeliads make ideal subjects for indoor culture. Brightly coloured leaves and vividly coloured flower spikes that can last for up to months at a time can make an eyecatching focal point for a room. Leaves are often more resistant to damage and more tolerant of dry air than many other houseplants and being slow-growing do not suddenly make long spindly growth as with many fast-growing types of plant. This said, the light conditions of a room or windowsill are often completely different to that of a greenhouse or conservatory. Choose those types which are more tolerant of low temperatures and drier air. The hybrids and species of billbergia, species of aechmea such as *A. fasciata* and neoregelia are ideal. Smaller species such as cryptanthus, tillandsia and the upright rosettes of *Billbergia nutans* can be grown on a windowsill. Don't forget that temperatures on windowsills can fluctuate wildly particularly during

29

winter and it may pay to find a new spot for them during this period.

Species that require lower light intensities such as guzmania and vriesia can also be grown in a room as long as the higher minimum temperatures of 60°F (15°C) can be maintained.

Light conditions can be improved by using supplementary lighting over the plants. These special bulbs produce a light spectrum which more mirrors that of natural daylight than the light bulbs we use to illuminate our rooms. They come in a variety of power sizes and with special fittings with built in reflectors which are suspended over the plants with chain link.

'Grolux' fluorescent tubes are a popular type of supplementary lighting which can be fitted beneath shelving or suspended freely in the air. Besides providing better light conditions, they have a low surface temperature and can be placed close to the leaves of the plants without fear of scorching.

Cultivation

In their native habitat, bromeliads inhabit a wide range of environmental situations, from growing on the ground to precariously taking root on trees and bushes. Successful cultivation relies on a basic knowledge of these specific requirements and mirroring, as far as possible, the general conditions that they experience in the wild.

Epiphytes
Many of the more unusual members of the bromeliad family are those that have evolved the capability of being able to grow up among the branches of lofty tropical trees and shrubs as epiphytes. Of the whole group, the grey-leaved tillandsias, commonly known as 'air-plants', are the most well known.

They have taken this mode of life to the extreme and can often be found in the wild clinging on to the thinnest of twigs with their tough wiry roots. They obtain their moisture almost exclusively from dew and mists which is absorbed by the scales which clad the leaves and give the plants their grey or silvery coloration.

They are frequently found for sale glued to ornamental bases such as sea shells, but the best way to grow them is to secure them to chunks of cork bark, obtainable from florists and garden centres, which can then be suspended using hooks or wires or placed on a windowsill. If purchasing your plants loose, find a specimen that has an existing root system. More often than not many will have been broken off in transit. Nestle the root system into a crevice in the bark and tie the plant carefully in place with thin nylon fishing line. Alternatively use a dab of silicone adhesive on an outer leaf. Sphagnum moss can also be wrapped around the roots of the plants to encourage further rooting. Unable to absorb much water via the roots the plants will require misting over with water at least once a day during the summer months but less during winter. Always use rainwater or soft tap water whenever possible. Rainwater can be collected in rain butts and there are now devices which can be fitted to the downpipe from the roof gutter. Periodic immersion in rainwater will also be very beneficial.

In summer, the plants can be hung outdoors in a warm sheltered spot. This is how they are cultivated at Heidelberg University in Germany, where they can be exposed to direct sun and summer rainfall.

Even air-plants require food to keep them healthy and encourage growth. They are best fed with a balanced liquid fertiliser. This is best applied from a handsprayer every third watering in summer and just occasionally during winter. Avoid using fertilisers high in nitrogen as this will encourage weak growth.

The smaller species can also be grown in terrariums and other small glass containers such as an empty sweet jar. Attached to slender but stout twigs, they can be inserted inside to create a miniature jungle scene. Dwarf terrestrial species such as cryptanthus could be planted in the bottom.

Growing in pots

Although nestling in the crotches of tree branches, most of the larger types of bromeliads such as aechmea, billbergia and guzmania can be successfully grown in pots.

In the wild they root into pockets of decaying leaf matter and although some eventually make quite large plants, the rootball tends to remain characteristically small or sparse but extremely tough. As a result, plants can remain in small pots for considerable periods of time with adequate feeding. Compost requirements reflect that used for orchids or cacti rather than that for general houseplants. It should be open and porous but while allowing excess moisture to drain away, still retaining sufficient to keep roots moist.

Most bromeliads can be grown in a mixture of equal parts medium sphagnum moss peat and coarse sand or horticultural grit. For extra drainage mix in a portion of pine bark chips, now available from a wide number of garden centres. Add a little slow-release base fertiliser such as bone meal to act as an ever constant supply of food.

Specific plant requirements will be covered in all the relevant species lists.

Pot size and the material it is made from affects both stability and the amount of moisture required by the plant. Terracotta or clay pots are far heavier and, because they are porous, dry out far more rapidly than plastic. This makes them ideally suited to many types of bromeliad

31

Figure 2   A bench framework of 20 in (50 cm) × 10 in (25 cm) sawn hardwood. The bench top and lower shelf are made of galvanised 'weldmesh' panels cut to size. The panels need support at about 24 in (60 cm) intervals.

Figure 3   A bench made from galvanised steel fence panels anchored to the wall and supported by 20 in (50 cm) × 20 in (50 cm) sawn hardwood posts.

although plastic is widely used because of cheapness and convenience of use. Also ensure that any greenhouse staging is strong enough to stand the weight of a large number of clay pots.

When potting on a bromeliad, invert the plant and, cradling the neck between the fingers, gently knock it out of its pot.

Choosing a pot 2–3 in (5–7.5 cm) larger in size, pour a small amount of compost into the bottom. If using a clay pot, place a large pebble or piece of broken pot over the drainage hole first.

Adjust the position of the rootball in the pot until the top is about 1 in (2.5 cm) below the rim. Work in compost around the sides, bumping the pot on the bench occasionally to settle in the compost. Water the plant in and allow to drain.

Most bromeliads require infrequent potting once mature, although young plants and seedlings may require this annually for the first few years.

Allow the compost to dry out between waterings. Bromeliads suffer more from being kept too wet at the roots than when allowed to get too dry. Keep the compost barely moist in winter. As a general rule, the drier the plant the lower the temperatures that it can withstand. Many rosette types have a tank or reservoir produced in the centre by overlapping leaf bases. It is not a requirement of most that this is constantly kept topped up with water although it will do no harm if you do. Always try to use fresh rainwater for this purpose. In winter, if the temperature is likely to drop below 45°F (7°C), it is a good idea to tip water out of the rosettes as new growth can be damaged by low water temperatures. This results in a brown line appearing on the leaf blade as it grows out.

During the growing season, keep the air humid around the plants by misting the air and/or ground with water. Avoid splashing water onto the leaves in full sunlight as this can cause scorching.

Liquid fertilisers are also the most effective way of feeding potted bromeliads. Again use a balanced liquid feed watered onto the compost every third watering during the growing season. Do not feed in winter.

Terrestrial types

Many of these grow between rocks on hot dry slopes in the high Andes. Plants such as puya, hechtia, dyckia and abromeitiella are some of the largest and smallest members of the bromeliad family. Leaves may be covered in fine white hairs or thick and succulent. Most are tolerant of extreme drought and intense sunlight. In cultivation, therefore, they require a hot, sunny position and well-drained compost.

A mixture of John Innes No. 1, or seed and cutting compost, with a portion of horticultural grit or perlite will give them the root conditions that they prefer. Give little or no water during the winter months.

Making a Bromeliad Tree

One of the most effective ways of displaying your bromeliad collection is to emulate how they would actually grow in the wild. The scope of the display would obviously be determined by the amount of space available. Even in a confined space, though, a bromeliad tree would make an imposing feature.

Look out for materials on which to grow your plants, such as tree stumps or branches of fallen trees. Lumps of driftwood are often sold in garden centres and, although expensive, would readily lend themselves for use without the effort of cleaning.

Alternatively, you can build your own tree. This is created by hanging sections of cork bark over a chicken wire frame. Cork bark can be bought from florists and garden centres but if your aims are ambitious it might be worth buying a whole bundle of cork bark sections from a florist's wholesalers.

First of all construct your cylindrical framework of chicken wire. Secure the edges in place with twists of wire. Its a good idea to model the branch and trunk widths to the size of bark sections to reduce the amount of cutting. After modelling the framework to your requirements, ensure that it is firmly anchored to the ground. If the structure is designed to rest on its side then no further anchorage is required. For a freestanding tree, the base should be set in a concrete mould such as a large pot or half barrel to prevent its falling over. Fit the section of cork over the framework bonding the edges together with contact or silicone adhesive. Small chunks of cork can be cut to fill in any remaining gaps.

If required, the whole structure can be filled in with polymeric foam filler, such as that used for insulating cavity walls. Kits can be purchased from DIY stores and builders merchants.

Before starting ensure that all gaps are plugged or covered with polythene sheet to prevent foam from oozing out.

Mix the two chemicals together and pour into the framework. Difficult areas such as branch joints may require holes cut into the cork so that the liquid can be poured in more accurately. Alternatively, tree sections can be filled with foam as they are constructed.

Once set, remove or cut away any foam which has oozed out of the holes and paint the surfaces buff to match the cork or alternatively fill the holes with sphagnum moss.

When using foam filler ensure that the manufacturer's instructions are followed carefully and ensure that there is free ventilation at all times while the job is underway.

Once completed, the tree can be planted up. Larger rosette-forming plants such as billbergia or neoregelia will require pockets of compost in which to grow. These can be made by bonding curved chunks of bark onto the main trunk. The larger and heavier plants are best placed on the main trunk so that the tree does not become unstable.

Pack the pockets with compost mixed with a little sphagnum moss. Insert the plants, working compost around the rootball. Until established, plants may require to be tied in place. Vigorous species are best planted as smaller specimens and allowed to grow on. Smaller epiphytic types will survive with sphagnum moss wrapped around their roots, held in place with a few turns of fishing line. The whole bundle can then be fixed to the branches using more nylon line. Grey-leaved tillandsias can be fixed to the tips of the branches again using line or a spot of silicone adhesive.

Plant up your tree as naturally as possible. Clusters of similar tillandsias will look far more effective than a number of different species dotted around the trunk. For an even more dramatic effect, introduce other epiphytic plants such as hoyas or rhipsalis. Climbers such as *Philodendron scandens* or *Scindapsus aureus* could be allowed to climb up the tree from a pot placed at the base. Water the tree and the plants on it with a handsprayer. Keeping the tree bark moist will help to maintain humidity.

Take care when watering plants placed in pockets as the compost can easily be washed out.

Bromeliads can also be grown in permanent displays. Troughs and tubs should be filled with a layer of coarse gravel or pebbles. Add the compost and plant up with the desired species. Large rosette types such as aechmeas can be used for the focal point. Smaller species such as cryptanthus can be used to underplant the scheme. Ferns and other tropical plants could be introduced to add further interest.

Many bromeliads also make excellent subjects for growing in hanging baskets or wall-mounted mangers. For the finishing touch, other epiphytic trailing plants can be allowed to cascade over the edge.

Summer displays

Although not frost hardy, bromeliads such as billbergia can be placed outdoors in the summer months without harm.

Grouped in association with many other types of potted plants, they will give your patio a tropical air. To prevent their blowing over in the wind, they can be set inside a larger pot filled with gravel.

In windy or very dry weather do not forget to keep the plants sprayed over with water.

Pests and diseases

In general, bromeliads remain remarkably free from pests and diseases. To prevent collections from becoming infected, always buy your plants from reputable nurseries. Endeavour to give them the conditions they require and get into the habit of checking them over as often as possible. Neglected plants in poor conditions will soon succumb to any unwelcome pest or disease.

Scale insects

Scale insects are the most serious threat to a bromeliad collection. They appear as small, straw-coloured limpet-like discs closely pressed on the leaf surface. The young insects move about freely and soon spread from plant to plant. Mature adults eventually become static to produce more young.

Left unchecked, they soon cover the whole plant making it look very unsightly. They feed by sucking sap, which causes small yellow blotches to appear on the lower leaf surface. A bad infestation of insects will soon weaken the plant.

Once identified, isolate any infected plants from the rest of the collection. A small number of individual insects can be picked off with a cocktail stick or crushed with a thumbnail. Well established infestations are best killed by chemical means. Those which kill on contact are not as effective as systemic insecticides. These are preparations which enter the sap stream of the plant, poisoning pests as they feed. A number of treatments throughout the year will be required to keep the infestation under control. Badly affected plants should be destroyed.

Mealy bug and root mealy bug

The other major pest is the mealy bug and root mealy bug. These resemble small, white woodlice about ¼ in (6 mm) long, which again feed off sap and soon make large colonies from eggs laid in characteristic fluffy balls of wool. Root mealy bug is more difficult to spot, hiding as it does amongst roots and at the base of the stem in dark crevices.

Small infestations can be controlled by using methylated spirits brushed onto the pests and their eggs.

Again spray the plants with malathion or a systemic insecticide, used at regular intervals according to the manufacturer's instructions.

For root mealy bug the chemicals should be drenched into the compost.

Red spider mite

Not a frequent problem, but these tiny buff-coloured insects will sometimes attack soft-leaved plants such as guzmania and vriesia. These pests can only be seen with a hand lens and colonise the undersides of the leaf. They again feed on sap and their feeding habits create a distinctive yellow speckling to the leaf. Eventually the plant is severely weakened. In advanced attacks, the mites produce a fine webbing on which they mass to be blown onto new sources of food. They thrive in hot, dry conditions, so raising the humidity and spraying over plants will suppress the spread.

Both contact and systemic insecticides will give control but red spider mite quickly becomes resistant to prolonged use of one particular chemical. A variety of chemicals used over the season will give more reliable results.

Diseases

Bromeliads are thankfully not affected by many diseases. Seedlings may be attacked by grey mould or botrytis if air conditions get too cold and stagnant. Young plants may also rot due to a damping-off fungus attacking the roots.

To avoid problems always use sterilised compost which is free-draining. Drench young seedlings with a fungicide to avoid trouble.

Disorders

A well-grown bromeliad is usually a healthy bromeliad. However, a sudden change or deterioration in growing conditions will eventually manifest itself in the appearance of the plant.

As a general rule, these plants can withstand hot, dry conditions far more effectively than those which are cold and wet. However, soft-leaved species may produce scorch marks on leaves when exposed to direct sunlight or shrivelled tips if left in dry air for prolonged periods of time.

In cold conditions reduce the humidity and tip out water from the centres of the rosettes if the temperature drops below 40°F (5°C) to prevent marking leaves. Water all plants sparingly in winter to prevent rotting roots.

Avoid spraying any compounds which contain oil on the leaves of those bromeliads which have absorbent scales as this will impair their activity and cause the plant to suffer.

The following is a checklist of problems which might sometimes be encountered.

Problem	Reason
Brown marks on leaves.	Watering in direct sun. Overwatering. Poor Drainage Light intensity too strong. Improper use of pesticides.
Leaves elongated (long and thin).	Not enough light. Too much nitrogen content in fertiliser.
Leaf tips brown (yellow).	Drainage inadequate. Too dry or cold. Not enough air movement. Alkaline water.
Leaves wilting.	Lack of water. Bad drainage.
Inner leaves sticking together (quilling).	No water in cup (reservoir) of plant. Excess pesticide dosage. Insufficient misting.
Bottom leaves yellow-brown (dying).	Characteristic of healthy plant which sheds older base leaves as it ages.
Bottom leaves brown at base.	Overwatering. Mixture too dense, bad drainage. Leaves embedded into mixture.

CHAPTER 5

AECHMEA

Figure 4   *Aechmea fasciata*

Their diversity of form, long-lasting flowering period and adaptability to cultivation make aechmeas possibly the most widely known and cultivated of all the bromeliad family. The attractive foliage, the long-lasting inflorescence and overall hardiness all serve to make them a most popular choice with growers.

This is a large genus with a geographical range covering an area from Central American and the West Indies to South America, extending as far south as Argentina.

The leaves may be banded or spotted with silver, black or maroon, all silver, so dark as to appear almost black, bicoloured with green above and wine red reverse, all wine red, soft shiny green, and heavily spined or hardly any spines at all. Some can grow quite large 5 ft (1.5 m) while others are quite small 1 ft (30 cm) with all sizes in between.

A minimum winter temperature of 45°F (7°C) is required for all species as long as they are kept dry. Those with thinner, more flexible leaves require a higher minimum of 50°F (10°C). They require bright light but should be shaded from direct sunlight to avoid scorching leaves.

Do not pot up too deeply and keep the mixture just damp. An open cymbidium orchid mixture suits very well. If potting the 'touchy' forms, a very 'chunky', well-drained mixture is required and just enough moisture to prevent dehydration during cold periods.

Try to keep the cups of the plants filled with water, particularly if they are mounted. In fact, it may be necessary to spray aechmeas at least once per day during very hot weather. Plants should be watered say twice a week in hot weather and once each week (or less) during the winter months. More or less watering depends on the conditions prevailing in the particular growing area and some experimentation may be necessary, keeping in mind not to overwater those that are grown in pots.

Aechmea fasciata and its varieties (Plates 1, 2), from Rio de Janeiro State and which are prevalent in the Organ Mountain region, are probably the best known and most widely grown of the aechmeas. The large, showy, pink, long-lasting bracts and blue petals changing to rose red as they age, never fail to captivate. It makes an excellent indoor pot plant and also adapts very easily to mounting either on driftwood or old stumps, especially those with horizontal limbs and rough, permanent bark.

Plants in the *Aechmea recurvata* group may change to fiery red as blooming approaches. This species from south Brazil, Uruguay, Argentina and Paraguay requires full sun for best form and foliage colour and is ideal for pot culture. The miniature *Aechmea recurvata* var. *benrathii* is spectacular as is *Aechmea recurvata* and var. *ortgiesii*. The many clones and hybrids of these species have long flowering periods, often lasting many months.

Aechmea orlandiana and *Aechmea fosteriana* from Espirito Santo in central-east coastal Brazil grow particularly well as mounted subjects; in fact they seem to have a preference for this form of culture. *Aechmea orlandiana* in particular shows its glorious banded foliage at its richest if grown this way. The Mulford Foster hybrid *Aechmea* 'Bert', with the above as parents, also is at its best when mounted. All have tough clinging woody stolons and grip their support in a few short weeks.

Aechmea orlandiana 'Ensign' with its tender variegated leaves is better mounted and under cover during the colder months.

Beautiful but touchy **Aechmea chantinii** (Plate 5) and its cultivars from Amazonian Peru, Amazonian Brazil, Colombia, Ecuador and Venezuela can be established on a suitable wood piece as an alternative to pot culture, and given overhead protection when required. The plant base and root area will have excellent air circulation, preventing base rot which can happen if these plants are deprived of winter warmth and have to cope with too much moisture in an unsuitable potting medium.

Aechmea chantinii is a variable species in size and colour. The foliage of some plants is green, in others it may be dark red to almost black. The leaves may range in length from 1–3 ft (30–90 cm) and the banding may be silver, dark green or almost black. The long, pendent bracts which hang below the erect, branched inflorescence can vary from orange to bright red; the flower petals are red and yellow.

Another for the bromeliad tree, log or stump is **Aechmea nudicaulis** (Plate 3) and its many forms. The sharp red and yellow inflorescence of the more widely grown forms never fails to attract attention in late spring. *Aechmea nudicaulis* has a wide habitat distribution and is extremely variable in size, foliage colour and inflorescence shades and form. It blooms regularly and will produce offsets if given space.

The gentle **Aechmea gamosepala** from south Brazil is perfect in dappled light. It is quite showy with its blue petals on cerise berries, the latter lasting for up to twelve months. Beautiful and with few spines on the soft green foliage, this would have to be one of the easiest species of the *Aechmea* genus.

For a dash of bright yellow petals and long-lasting orange berries, **Aechmea caudata** (Plate 4), **Aechmea comata** and **Aechmea calyculata** from south Brazil are very easy to grow. *Aechmea caudata* var. *cipperi*, the blue-flowered *caudata* form with its burnt-orange berries on a branched spike, is most attractive and again ideally grown in medium to bright, filtered light.

Soft-leaved aechmeas, *victoriana, victoriana* var. *discolor, racinae, warasii, fulgens* var. *discolor, miniata, miniata* var. *discolor* and others, require more shade and should be protected against direct sunlight. They also make excellent houseplants back from a well-lit window.

Bicoloured, soft-leaved aechmeas especially seem to adapt very readily to indoor culture. Although light is always beneficial to any living plant, these seem to tolerate less light than most.

The popular hybrids *Aechmea* 'Royal Wine' (Mulford Foster cross using *Aechmea miniata* var. *discolor* and *Aechmea victoriana* var. *discolor*) and *Aechmea* 'Foster's Favorite' (cross using *Aechmea victoriana* var. *discolor* and *Aechmea racinae*), have proven their adaptability to indoor culture over the years. The latter has an upright rosette of shiny, deep maroon leaves. The pendent inflorescence has coral petals tipped with blue. *Aechmea* 'Foster's Favorite Favorite' is a variegated form.

Aechmea gracilis with pronounced stolons and branched inflorescence with blue petals and long-lasting berries, is an ideal subject for a basket. The small clone is particularly useful for this form of culture.

Aechmea bracteata from Central America with shapely urn form and showy, prominent spines is quite easy to grow in a bright position. It has a long-lasting, branched spike with red scape, yellow petals and green berries that eventually turn black. Though chiefly spiny the urn varieties are an interesting addition to any collection.

The flowers of many are generally in 'cob' form and the petals quickly turn to black berries but the pink to deep red scape and scape bracts have great eye appeal. All require bright light but not all can cope with full sun. Most are from the mountain regions of east Brazil and the sun does not have the same searing rays as experienced at lower altitudes. Many have a silver haze to the leaves in habitat but lose it when taken out of their natural environment. *Aechmea chlorophylla* is one which retains the silver foliage if grown in good light or full, humid sun.

The species *Aechmea triangularis* is not a large plant but is heavily spined. The more intense the light the better the shape and foliage appeal. Under the right conditions this plant grows squat with golden foliage and has touches of red on the tips of the leaves which seem to fold back, each forming a triangle. With its beautiful spike with red scape and purple petals on cob bracts which change to black berries, *triangularis* always commands attention.

Possibly the largest of the urn-form aechmeas in cultivation is *Aechmea leucolepis* from the state of Bahia in mid-northern coastal Brazil. Not colourful with its green 'cob' inflorescence, this plant can look beautiful if conditioned to full sun and the barrel form in golden-green makes *Aechmea leucolepis* certainly interesting.

There seem unlimited ways to cultivate and enjoy this genus and with several hundred known species and many worthwhile hybrids available, a collection of aechmeas alone would provide endless pleasure.

The following are a few more which you may find in specialist nurseries.

Aechmea dichlamydea var. trinitensis is a large, beautiful plant which attains a height of about 3 ft (90 cm) and a diameter of about 3½ ft

(110 cm) when in flower. It has grey-green leaves and a multi-branched inflorescence of blue and coral. The flowers are white and lilac which later turn into deep blue berries. It needs a warm tropical environment to be successful and would be hard to grow without a heated glasshouse.

Aechmea ramosa is a medium to large-sized plant, with apple-green leaves edged with dark spines. With very bright light the foliage can become flushed with rose-pink. A large, branched, greenish-yellow flower head with rose-coloured bracts is followed by green berries.

Aechmea ramosa var. rubra is the same as above but is a larger plant, and the leaves are dusky pink which can turn to a copper colour in good light.

Aechmea weilbachii var. weilbachii. The apple-green leaves form a medium-sized rosette. The tall, arching inflorescence is red with orange ovaries and lilac petals which soon turn to black.

CHAPTER 6

ANANAS

Figure 5   *Ananas comosus* var. *variegata*

These bromeliads belong to the subfamily Bromelioideae and are terrestrially grown in both high and low altitudes in Brazil. Included is the common commercial pineapple, the decorative types with smaller fruits and the coloured, variegated specimens, all of which can be grown successfully in greenhouses, conservatories or indoors as a houseplant. They require warm conditions and a minimum temperature of 60°F (15°C).

Their stiff, serrated leaves form a somewhat loose but dense rosette, and they have an obvious scape with a cone-shaped (or strobiliform) inflorescence crowned with a tuft of sterile, leaf-like bracts, and petals which are mauve to red.

Ananas ananassoides, a small ornamental species grown terrestrially, is native to the semi-arid regions of eastern and northern Brazil, Paraguay, Bolivia, Argentina and Venezuela at altitudes of 200–1350 m, and generally in drier areas than other species of ananas are found. The erect flower stem with reddish bracts holds the colourful purple or red fruit 6 in (15 cm) long which, although edible, is not particularly flavoursome and is full of seeds.

Ananas bracteatus (plate 9) has a wide distribution in coastal areas of Brazil, especially from the foothills to the mountains, reaching altitudes of around 300–400 m. Also a lover of extremely bright light, this large attractive plant usually has red foliage and bears the stunning scarlet fruit which develops at maturity to earn this species the name 'red pineapple'. Two much sought after variegated forms of this plant are *Ananas bracteatus* var. *tricolor* and *Ananas bracteatus* var. *striatus* (Plate 10.

Ananas comosus is the edible and most commonly known form of pineapple, and although it appears to have originated in central Brazil, it is now grown in vast numbers by commercial pineapple growers in most tropical climates throughout the world. When fully grown, the plant of *Ananas comosus* is much too large for cultivation as a houseplant, and it needs direct full sun to develop that golden-yellow pineapple with which we are so familiar.

A more desirable horticultural form suitable for indoor or outdoor cultivation is the beautiful *Ananas comosus* var. *variegatus* which, when grown in very high light, including direct sunlight, produces attractive ivory and green, longitudinal-striped leaves suffused with rose-pink tonings which become deeper when the plant is exposed to sufficient bright light or sunlight.

This magnificent variegated plant with its scarlet red pineapple is much admired in cultivation. The fruit normally develops from that portion of the stalk which has borne flowers; it thickens to form a bright red pineapple that lasts for several months, after which the tufted leafhead can be cut from the completely ripened fruit, stripped of the lower leaves and planted in a pot with a well-draining medium such as cymbidium orchid mixture. At the same time, any 'suckers' or offsets which appear from the base of the fruit or at the base of the plant or from between the leaf pockets may (when they reach mature size) be carefully removed, potted and placed in bright light, keeping them just damp. As many as three or four suckers may be found at the base of the fruit.

Ananas fritzmuelleri is a large variety found in woods of south-eastern Brazil from São Paulo to Santa Catarina at low elevations.

Ananas lucidus is native to Amazonian Brazil, Venezuela, Guiana and Peru. The erect, bright green leaves (approximately 3 ft [90 cm] long) become pinkish when exposed to bright light, and are spineless except for a long terminal spine. The fruit is small and attractive, and consumed mainly by natives although it is lacking in delicate flavour. In the West Indies it was introduced for the strong fibre produced by the leaves.

Ananas monstrosus is native to Amazonas, Brazil. This species does not have the 'top knot' or coma on top of the inflorescence.

Ananas nanus is a dwarf ornamental species found from arid cooler regions of central Brazil to northern inland Brazil at altitudes of approximately 500 m in open forest areas. This quaint plant grows about 18 in (45 cm) tall, and although it requires only a 4 in (10 cm) pot, will mature and bear flowers and a hard, dark-green fruit atop an 18 in (45 cm) tall stem which rises from the centre of a rosette of deeply arched, dark-green leaves. The fruit, although inedible, has a distinct pineapple fragrance. This species is known to produce numerous offsets, a characteristic quite inconsistent with most plants of the *Ananas* genus.

Ananas parguazensis is found in Amazonian Brazil, Colombia, Venezuela and Surinam in hot, humid areas.

The mono-generic ***Pseudananas sagenarius***, formerly known as *macrodontes*, is also without the coma or 'top knot' and offsets on long stolons. This is found in dense forests from sea level to the mountain regions of southern Brazil, Paraguay, Peru, south-eastern Bolivia and Ecuador.

All ananas species thrive in a moist, well-drained potting medium (not constantly wet), and full sunlight or extremely bright indoor light, in temperatures of 60°F (16°C) upwards. During summer they need water two to three times a week depending on local conditions. In winter they can be 'touchy' and should be watered very sparingly.

CHAPTER 7

BILLBERGIA

Figure 6   *Billbergia* × *windii*

The genus *Billbergia* contains some of the most commonly grown bromeliads, such as *Billbergia nutans* and *Billbergia pyramidalis* var. *concolor*.

Billbergias are native to Eastern Brazil, Mexico and Central America in the main, but have been found in Peru and Argentina. They are epiphytes and in their natural habitat are found usually in large clumps growing in good light. Some plants do fall to the ground and grow very well, adapting to a terrestrial habit without difficulty.

The genus *Billbergia* is divided into two subgenera, Billbergia and Helicodea, and most of the cultivated species belong to the first subgenus. Helicodeas are called the 'watch spring' billbergias because their flower petals recurve and coil a number of times like a watch spring. The petals of the subgenus Billbergia recurve after the flower opens, but do not coil on themselves.

Billbergias were among the first bromeliads to be hybridised, mainly because they are easy to flower and their floral parts are easily seen and manipulated. Consequently many of those now grown are hybrids.

In horticulture billbergias are generally easy to grow. However, most require high light and unless given such conditions, tend to become strappy and of straggling growth. With enough light, the majority form tight tubes, frequently with silver crossbands. A few species need some shade.

Containers

Billbergias are very adaptable to terrestrial culture and can be grown successfully in just about any container, including pots made of plastic, terracotta or concrete, timber boxes, or wire baskets lined with moss.

Mixture

Due to the epiphytic nature of this genus, any open compost that is 'light', free-draining, and stable enough to support the plant, will produce good results. Cymbidium orchid potting mixture is suitable.

Light

If there is one thing that the majority of billbergias will not tolerate, it is not enough light. To achieve the best results with most of these plants strong light is required, and if desired they can even be grown in full sun by gradually acclimatising them to this.

Water and Humidity

These plants are best grown 'hard'. The potting medium should be kept fairly dry and the plants misted every few days to maintain a humidity level between 30 and 50 per cent.

Temperature

The low point of the scale is of major importance. Billbergias will tolerate high temperatures, but as for most bromeliads temperatures below 45°F (7°C) for long periods of time can be disastrous.

Fertilising

A liquid fertiliser suitable for orchids but at half the strength shown on the container, applied to the potting medium at monthly intervals, can be beneficial. Some growers prefer not to use fertiliser and others take the opposite view, so experiment and see which works best for you.

Billbergia Species

The following is a list of billbergia species generally available. The two subgenera have been listed separately. A final listing contains billbergia hybrids.

Subgenus Billbergia

Billbergia amoena is one of the commonest species. Mostly tubular and often tinged with red, some forms are green and may be more open in shape. The inflorescence is usually upright with bright red (or orange) bracts. The sepals and petals are green and may or may not have blue tips. Varieties include *rubra* (Plate 11), *viridis*, *penduliflora* and *stolonifera*, the latter producing new plants at the end of stolons which may be up to 3¼ ft (1 m) long.

Billbergia brasiliensis (Plate 12) is a large, tightly tubular rosette about 3 ft (90 cm) in height. The broad leaves are silver-banded and the plant has a large, pendulous inflorescence. The bracts are red and the petals dark blue.

Billbergia chlorosticta (syn. Billbergia saundersii) has a small tubular rosette of few leaves which are usually red pigmented with numerous white spots. The inflorescence is simple with red bracts, red sepals and green petals with blue tips. This species has often been used as a parent in hybridisation.

Billbergia distachia (Plate 13) A silvery, small, fat tube with an inflorescence which is quite similar to *Billbergia nutans* except that the green flowers do not have blue edges, although they often have blue tips. It is like *Billbergia nutans* also in that it is very easy to grow.

Billbergia euphemiae, a small tubular rosette, propagates on stolons about 4 in (10 cm) long. This type is green with silver bands, while the variety *purpurea* has deep red (plum) undersides to the leaves and a much more open rosette. The inflorescence is pendulous with pale pink sepals and green petals. Various amounts of blue occur on the tips. The variety *purpurea* has been popular as a parent.

Billbergia fosteriana. This species is unusual in that it forms a tall, up to 2½ ft (75 cm) high, very narrow tube composed of only two or three leaves. It is very silvery and has faint crossbands. The inflorescence is erect, mealy white, and is relatively few-flowered. The petals are green with blue tips. It is most closely related to *Billbergia macrocalyx*, and is not a common plant in cultivation.

Billbergia horrida. This attractive billbergia may have green to red pigmented leaves which have quite large, dark spines. The tube is usually well marked with silver crossbands. The inflorescence is distinctive in that it is upright, with very pale silvery green-yellow flowers tightly clustered at the top. The flower petals have very pale blue tips. The variety *tigrina* has deep red-brown leaves.

Billbergia leptopoda (Plate 15) has a small tube with green leaves which have numerous white spots. The plant is sometimes called 'Permanent Wave' because the ends of the leaves turn right back and coil on themselves. The inflorescence is somewhat decurved or upright and the petals are green with blue tips.

Billbergia macrocalyx is quite large growing, up to 2¼ ft (70 cm) high with a few-leaved green tube which has white crossbands. The inflorescence is upright, mealy white, and the flowers have green petals with blue at the tips and along the edges.

Billbergia nutans is a very small, about 8 in (20 cm) high, tight tube made of two to three leaves. The inflorescence is nodding with bright pink bracts. The flowers have pink sepals and the petals are green with blue tips and edges. This is one of the easiest species to grow.

Billbergia pyramidalis. The leaves of this species are green, sometimes with silver banding. The inflorescence is upright and the flowers are densely packed. In var. *concolor* the petals are red, whereas in var. *pyramidalis* they are red with blue tips.

Billbergia sanderiana now includes *Billbergia chlorantha* and *Billbergia* *elegans*. The leaves are green with various amounts of purple pigment, particularly towards the base of the leaves. The leaves bear very large black spines which are a feature of this plant. The rosette is loosely tubular and the inflorescence is completely pendulous, sometimes hanging down below the base of the plant. The bracts are pink but unfortunately fade quickly. The petals are green with blue tips.

Billbergia vittata was one of the first bromeliads introduced into horticulture. It has a tall, tight, grey tube with marked silver bands. The inflorescence is pendulous with orange bracts and violet flowers.

Subgenus Helicodea

Billbergia alfonsi-johannis has a squat tube which is almost without markings. The leaves are broad and leathery and bear large spines. the pendulous inflorescence is typical of this subgenus, having very large pink bracts and a very elongated section bearing the flowers which are greenish-yellow. The whole inflorescence is one of the largest in the genus.

Billbergia decora has the most attractive tube of this group. It is tall (up to 2 ft [60 cm]) and brown-grey in colour with conspicuous silver crossbands. The inflorescence is pendent, silvery, bears large, pink bracts and the flowers have greenish petals.

Billbergia meyeri is different from most of the others in this list in that the tube is very narrow (about 1–1½ in [2–3 cm] wide) although quite tall. It is brown-grey in colour with irregular crossbands. The inflorescence is pendulous with pink bracts (which fade quickly) and greenish petals.

Billbergia porteana is a large-growing Brazilian species with a green leathery tube up to 3¼ ft (1 m) or more high. The tube has irregular and somewhat inconspicuous silver bands. Again the inflorescence is pendulous, sometimes reaching the base of the plant. It has large pink bracts and the flowers have green petals.

Billbergia venezuelana (syn. Billbergia rosea) (Plate 16), like the previous species is a large plant with a tube more than 3¼ ft (1 m) high. It is brownish in colour with good silver crossbands. The pendulous inflorescence is very large with pink bracts and gold-green petals.

Billbergia zebrina (Plate 17) is the commonest species of this group in cultivation. Plants under various names turn out to be forms of this common Brazilian species. Generally it has leathery green leaves with brownish pigment and varying amounts of silver crossbanding. The tube is about 20–27 in (50–70 cm) high. Like the other species it has a pendulous inflorescence with large pink bracts and gold-coloured petals. The seed capsules are large, silvery and turban shaped.

Billbergia Hybrids

There are a large number of billbergia hybrids, some of them raised many years ago. Some of the best known are:

Billbergia 'Catherine Wilson' (*Billbergia amoena viridis* × *Billbergia iridifolia*) This hybrid has a very attractive, narrow, pinkish tube which bears numerous cream blotches. The inflorescence has pink bracts and green and blue flowers. Again it has been used to produce further hybrids.

Billbergia 'Fantasia' (*Billbergia saundersii* × *Billbergia pyramidalis*) This is a rather famous hybrid raised by Mulford Foster. The tube is somewhat open, and has green leaves with many cream spots and blotches. The inflorescence has reddish bracts and red and blue flowers.

Billbergia 'Fascinator' (*Billbergia saundersii* × *Billbergia windii*) This plant is similar to 'Fantasia' but the tubes are pigmented reddish-brown as well as having numerous cream blotches. It does not flower freely but has brilliant red bracts and blue flowers. The plant is not as subject to cold damage as 'Fantasia'.

Billbergia 'Muriel Waterman' (*Billbergia horrida* var. *tigrina* × *Billbergia euphemiae var. purpurea*) This plant has a leathery red tube with silver crossbands. The inflorescence has pink bracts and numerous blue flowers. It has been used further as a parent.

CHAPTER 8

CRYPTANTHUS

Figure 7   *Cryptanthus bromelioides* var. *tricolor*

Cryptanthus are small, star-shaped plants with a symmetrical or oval form and distinctive flattish leaves. There are about 50 species and many hybrids in cultivation.

They are terrestrial in habitat and come mainly from Brazil where they grow under widely varying conditions; in sun and shade, in moist and dry areas, in coastal regions and forests. However, under cultivation they seem to grow best where they have bright light, warmth and humidity.

Most species and hybrids are low spreading rosettes with about ten to twelve leaves 2–12 in (5–30 cm) in length. The leaves tend to be crinkled, especially on the edges, and often mottled and striped with many unusual colours, such as brown, rose, silver, copper, grey, light green, pink, white and red or a combination of these colours. Most cryptanthus have white flowers that barely emerge from the centre of the plants, so that they are considered to be foliage plants rather than flowering plants. As the leaves are quite beautiful, and because of their small size, they can make good container arrangements for indoors or in a terrarium or old fish tank.

Cryptanthus in their natural habitat are true terrestrials and a few are saxicolous (growing on rocks). They have never been observed as epiphytes and should not be mounted on wood or bark. They should not be underpotted, for they develop a root system at least equal to the size of the plant, if well grown. A 5 in (13 cm) plastic pot is suggested to help conserve the moisture the plant requires.

The potting medium should be loose and porous. If possible, this should never be allowed to dry out totally. In winter less water will be required, and if the plants are kept in a cold environment very little water should be given. Keep in mind that whatever mix is used, it must be kept damp for the best growth. Cryptanthus do very well in self-watering pots, or in pots sitting on capillary matting. You can also stand them in a dish of water during very hot weather and refill when needed.

Although it is not necessary to fertilise in order to have a beautiful display of colour and unusual markings, you should fertilise to obtain maximum growth. Cryptanthus are not very fussy about the fertiliser, but use it in diluted form, about half to quarter of the recommended strength. Any balanced fertiliser works well, or a slow-release granular fertiliser combined with the potting mix for newly planted offsets shows good results. Many cryptanthus fanciers fertilise with each watering using an extremely dilute solution. The point is, they like to be fed and the amount of fertiliser really depends on the intensity of light in which the plant is grown; the more light, the more feeding that can be undertaken.

There are cryptanthus which will grow in any light conditions you may have. For example, *Cryptanthus beuckeri* is a low-light plant and many of its hybrids also like to be shaded, in humid conditions, therefore these make good terrarium plants. Others such as *Cryptanthus bahianus*, *Cryptanthus 'Rubra', Cryptanthus 'Cascade' and *Cryptanthus warasii*

1 *Aechmea fasciata*

2 *Aechmea fasciata* var. *variegata*

3 *Aechmea nudicaulis*

4 *Aechmea caudata* var. *variegata*

5 *Aechmea chantinii*

6 *Aechmea lueddemanniana* 'Mend'

7 *Aechmea pectinata* in habitat

8 *Aechmea pectinata*

9 *Ananas bracteatus* fruit

10 *Ananas bracteatus* var. *striatus*

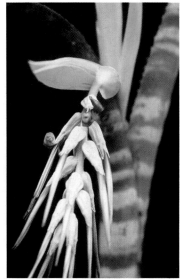

11 *Billbergia amoena* var. *rubra*

12 *Billbergia brasiliensis*

13 *Billbergia distachia*

14 *Billbergia euphemiae* var. *purpurea*

15 *Billbergia leptopoda*

16 *Billbergia venezuelana*

17 *Billbergia zebrina*

18 *Cryptanthus* 'Pink Starlight'

19 *Guzmania lingulata*

20 *Guzmania gloriosa*

21 *Neoregelia carolinae 'Meyendorfii albo-marginata'*

22 *Neoregelia carolinae 'Meyendorfii variegata'*

23 *Neoregelia carolinae 'Meyendorfii albo-marginata'*

24 *Neoregelia marmorata*

25 *Neoregelia* 'Painted Desert'

26 *Nidularium billbergioides* var. *citrinum*

27 *Nidularium billbergioides*

28 *Nidularium fulgens*

29 *Nidularium innocentii* var. *wittmackianum*

30 *Tillandsia fasciculata*

31 *Tillandsia filifolia* 'Tree'

32 *Tillandsia mauryana*

33 *Tillandsia magnusiana*

34 *Tillandsia xerographica*

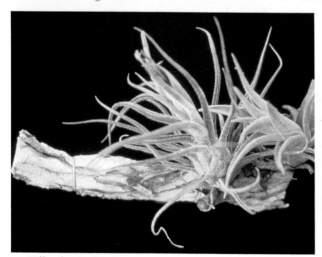

35 *Tillandsia pruinosa*

36 *Tillandsia streptophylla*
inflorescence

37 *Vriesea platynema*

38 *Vriesea fosteriana*

39 *Vriesea psittacina*

40 *Bromelia balansae*

41 *Vriesea scalaris*

42 *Streptocalyx poeppigii* inflorescence

43 *Streptocalyx holmesii*

can take full sun but you will find the plants happier in diffused light. For maximum colour in most cryptanthus, bright diffused light is necessary. Too much light will cause bleached spots on the foliage or a leathery look to the plants. In extreme cases sunburnt spots or even holes will occur. On the other hand weak foliage and greening of the colour suggests the plant needs more light. Acclimatise your plants to grow in as much light as possible in the area you have set aside for them. A spot that is sheltered from the cold and winter rains would be desirable.

Cryptanthus require a minimum temperature of 60°F (15°C) as this produces the best growing conditions for them. Many survive in temperatures just above freezing if they are kept dry during winter, but it will not keep them looking their best, and they will require trimming and the new summer growth to recover some of their good looks. They can also take temperatures above 100°F (38°C) as long as there is good air circulation and the soil is not allowed to dry out.

Most species enjoy humid conditions. Plants grown inside require more attention to humidity as houses tend to have drier conditions than the greenhouse, especially during winter. Setting pots over water on capillary matting does a great deal to increase the humidity and maintain moisture for them. Cryptanthus will grow in well-lit bathrooms or above the kitchen sink where the humidity is generally greater.

Soon after the plants have bloomed and the flowers have dried up, offsets will be produced. These normally come from between the leaves, or from stolons, or from the base of the plant. These offsets may be left on the mother plant to continue growing to form a group of plants or they may be removed when they are about a quarter the size of the parent. Some plants release their offsets when they are sufficiently mature and the latter will come away from the mother plant when gently touched. Others may require a gentle tug or twist to release them.

The offsets usually do not have roots, although those from the base of the plant may do so if allowed to become fairly large. They will root easily in the potting mix. A dressing of root hormone powder seems to help but they will root without it, possibly more slowly, and in cooler weather it may take up to eight weeks for the offset to send out roots.

Make a small depression in the mix, insert the short stem, then press the mixture firmly around the young plant. Do not pot deeper than the base of the first leaf. Stake or secure the plant if necessary, to keep it from rocking back and forth. An elastic band of the appropriate size is quite useful for holding it in the mix. It is essential that the plant be secure to root well and make good growth. Place the plant in good growing conditions in semi-shade and water it. Move it into more light when it has rooted.

There are too many cryptanthus species and hybrids to describe them all, but the ones mentioned below will interest the beginner.

Cryptanthus acaulis is a small star-shaped rosette of undulating green leaves about 5 in (13 cm) across. In var. *argenteus*, the upper sides of the leaves are coated with silvery scales while in var. *ruber*, the leaves are tinged with red in bright light.

Cryptanthus beuckeri is a medium-sized plant with green and cream mottled, spoon-shaped leaves, that grow out and upward and are about 5–6 in (13–15 cm) long.

Cryptanthus bivittatus is a small grower to about 3 in (7.5 cm) and has longitudinal stripes of salmon-rose and olive-green on stiff, spiky leaves. It produces many offsets.

Cryptanthus bromelioides var. tricolor, medium size plant 14–18 in (35–45 cm) across, about 20 leaves that form an upright rosette of green and white, and which flush pink in bright light. Offshoots are produced on upright stolons near the base of the plant.

Cryptanthus 'Cascade' is a medium-sized plant which forms a reddish rosette in good light, with new plantlets growing on long stolons that can reach 2 ft (60 cm) in length. Suitable for hanging baskets.

Cryptanthus fosterianus, a large, striking plant with thick, stiff, brown leaves which have zigzag crossbands of contrasting grey and form a handsome flat rosette.

Cryptanthus 'It' is a large plant that forms a stiff rosette with variegated foliage of green, white and pink when grown in strong light.

Cryptanthus lacerdae, a very pretty small plant, has two silvery stripes on a green background, and rarely exceeds 4 in (10 cm) across.

Cryptanthus 'Pink Starlight' (Plate 18) is a small, tight rosette of white and pink leaves with an olive-green stripe down the centre of them. This dainty plant seldom grows more than 6 in (15 cm) across.

Cryptanthus 'Ti' is a medium to large plant that forms a rosette of rose-coloured leaves edged with a stripe of dark grey-green.

Cryptanthus zonatus is a medium to large, handsome plant with undulating green leaves which have silver-grey zigzag crossbands. It forms a flat, low-growing rosette, about 10–12 in (25–30 cm) across.

CHAPTER 9

DYCKIA AND *HECHTIA*

Figure 8   *Dyckia*

Dyckia

Possibly the best known of the terrestrial genera, at a glance dyckias resemble yucca, howorthia, agave and others of the succulent family, but there the similarity ends. Although they are often grown by cacti and succulent collectors and enjoy similar culture, dyckias are unrelated and have a charm all their own.

With over 100 known species and a significant number of worthwhile hybrids, many with rich foliage shades often surpassing the beauty of their parents, there are dyckias in all colours and sizes to interest the gardener with a taste for something different. These sturdy xerophytic plants are native to South America where most are to be found in Brazil, chiefly the central and southern regions, and in lesser numbers in Paraguay, Bolivia, northern Argentina and Uruguay.

Dyckias range in size from miniatures of 2–3 in (5–7.5 cm) across to giants up to 5 ft (1.5 m) in diameter and every size in between. The stiff, spined foliage can be various shades of green, rose, maroon, tan, silver, and sometimes so heavily dusted with absorption scales, white, when viewed from a distance. Reliable spring bloomers, their flowers are bell-shaped on a long, simple or branched stem. The petals can be shades of yellow, orange through to red.

They are found at altitudes from sea level to 1500 m, often growing in rock crevices with roots nourished by humus washed down by rain. Sometimes found high on granite cliff faces in full tropical sun, or in tidal areas enjoying wet, and then almost dry conditions, or in open sunny scrublands as terrestrials exposed to all weather extremes.

Their hardiness and eye appeal with pleasing rosette form, adds interest to any mixed bromeliad collection. Given enough room, the eventual colonies become a talking point even during the non-blooming season. Basking in the sun and ignoring the cold once established, these interest-ing plants really take care of themselves. They can also be placed out on the patio in summer. Dyckias (particularly the miniatures) can even be grown indoors in a bright room, in decorative containers.

With the larger varieties thought must be given to container size as dyckias have a well-developed root system. Although not rapid growers, in a few years it may be necessary to pot on to a larger size before the plants have become potbound. If this stage is reached through neglect over the years, insufficient water during summer may cause damage to the terminal spines. This can spoil the appearance of an otherwise attractive colony.

Where space is a problem some of the delightful miniatures can be grown. These seldom outgrow their containers and can be moved around to chase the sunny areas during winter.

Like all bromeliads dyckias require a well-drained compost. Do not plant too deeply. It is sufficient to plant the root area only and firm it in. Use broken tiles, brick pieces or coarse grit to crock the pot. A suitable mixture is composed of coarse sand, gravel, damp peat moss and pine bark chips. An added boost of bone meal or slow-release pellets at the time of planting can be beneficial. However, the beauty of these plants is more evident if they are hard grown and not pampered.

If snails and slugs are prevalent it may be necessary to sprinkle some repellent during late winter to protect the developing spring flower spikes. It can be disappointing to lose the pleasure of their reliable blooming period through this oversight.

All dyckias like very bright light to full sun to reach their full potential. The rich foliage shades are evident if they are recognised as sun loving plants and treated accordingly. In their homelands dyckias enjoy average to hot temperatures during spring and summer 60–95°F (16–35°C) and autumn and winter 50–80°F (10–27°C). In their native homelands they grow in wet to almost dry conditions and receive moisture from high summer rainfall (the wet season) and constant humidity from night fogs and mists which sustain them during the drier months.

Special care must be given to the rare, extreme xerophytic form *Dyckia marnier-lapostollei*, named in honour of the French horticulturist Julien Marnier-Lapostolle. Collected high in the mountains of the central Brazilian state of Goias, clinging to rock cavities exposed to hot days and cold nights with excellent light and perfect drainage, this plant and similar varieties are not demanding, but a little extra thought must be given to their culture. It requires sunny well-ventilated conditions. The pot should just hold roots comfortably. It needs a very gritty, open mixture and needs to be kept barely damp during winter. With its thick, broad, velvety leaves heavily coated with absorption scales and slow-growing habit, this plant makes a treasured companion for cacti and succulents of similar culture.

Propagation of dyckias is easy provided their spine-edged leaves are treated with respect. Unless a variety with few spines is being divided, stout gloves are always necessary. It is more satisfactory to take the colony completely out of its container where space allows.

Some dyckia offsets or pups may already have roots, and can be potted up immediately. Provide a container large enough, but not too large, to accommodate the new plant's roots. Water carefully, until the plant has established.

Some dyckias are notorious for developing a colony of several crowns growing from a united base. These require dividing with a hacksaw or secateurs. All wounds must be dusted with fungicide or hormone rooting powder and allowed to callous. They are then planted using a gritty mixture of coarse sand and damp peat moss and watered sparingly until the roots develop. It is possible to lose new plants by rotting caused by overwatering during this period. Propagation by division generally presents no problems if handled during the warmer months.

Raising dyckias from seed is a fascinating challenge for the adventurous gardener and it is possible to grow them to flowering stage in about three years by potting on and light feeding. For details on this method refer to the section on propagation by seed in Chapter 16.

The following are a few of the dyckias met with in cultivation.

Dyckia brevifolia (meaning short-leaved) was discovered in south-eastern Brazil growing on rocks beside streams, experiencing hot dry conditions except during the rainy season when it is frequently submerged by floods. The stiff, open, broad-leaved rosettes are an attractive green and measure 5 in (12 cm) or less across in cultivation. This species is suitable for full sun. The attractive flowers are a rich yellow.

Dyckia choristaminea (meaning the stamens are not fused), is a dwarf species found growing in open rocky ground in south Brazil. With individual rosettes 3 in (7 cm) or less across, forming attractive mounds of grey-green, this is a very desirable container subject especially for growers with limited space. With leaves recurved, few spines and its attractive daffodil-yellow flowers on 'dwarf stems', this species has much to recommend it.

Dyckia fosteriana, from southern Brazil, is probably the most ornamental and popular species in cultivation with its almost aluminium sheen bronzing in full sun, the individual rosettes less than 1 in (2.5 cm) across and the flowers with deep yellow petals. Usually grown as a container subject and not as slow as the extreme xerophytes, *Dyckia fosteriana* can develop into a stunning colony in a few years.

Dyckia leptostachya (meaning thin-stemmed), is indigenous to southern and western Brazil, south-eastern Bolivia, Paraguay and north-eastern Argentina. Found growing in open scrubland. Not usually as heavily spined as many dyckias and though the rosettes can reach from 10–12 in (25–30 cm) across in cultivation, handling is not a problem. The interesting leaves, usually maroon, and broad at the base, taper to a long, whip-like point. This and the orange-red petals of its flowers makes this plant a delight. Underground stolons produce new plants and the usual offsets develop around the base of the parent plant.

Dyckia remotiflora (meaning flowers widely separated). With four varieties this species is found on dry, open, rocky ground at low elevations in southern Brazil, Uruguay and Argentina. Generally 4–6 in (10–15 cm) across in cultivation, with grey-green, recurved foliage and few spines. The tall stem carries flowers with deep orange petals. *Dyckia remotiflora* and its varieties is another gem of the genus.

Many hybrids have been created using *Dyckia fosteriana* and *Dyckia leptostachya*, the resulting foliage pigment usually a glorious deep maroon all year round. Using the species *Dyckia leptostachya* and *Dyckia brevifolia* hybrids form rugged slow-growing plants of medium-size in shades of pink-tan. Their form can favour either parent. The tall flower spikes have lemon-yellow petals.

Hechtia

A rugged member of the bromeliad family, hechtias are found growing in the arid regions of Texas, USA and the northern area of Central America.

With over 40 known species, the majority are indigenous to the desert areas of Mexico, clinging to rocky cliffs, thriving on desert hillsides and growing as terrestrials in dry scrubland with cacti and succulents.

True xerophytes, hechtias require less water but in other respects are of similar culture to dyckias. The flowers are produced on long, branched stems and the petals are usually white, occasionally pink.

Hechtias are heavily spined and exist in a size range, from 6 in–5 ft (15 cm–1.5 m) across. Plants of the smaller forms make interesting tub specimens for full sun.

Hechtia argentea (meaning silvery). This stunning plant from Central Mexico makes a large, slow-growing rosette composed of long, silvery spine-edged leaves. When mature, it produces a flower spike formed of many small, white flowers and light brown bracts. It is a plant of easy culture, given a well-drained compost, full sun and little water.

CHAPTER 10

GUZMANIA

Figure 9   *Guzmania* 'Memoria Louis Dutrie'

Guzmanias are not as numerous as tillandsias or vrieseas, but have among their numbers some of the aristocrats of the bromeliad family. They belong to the subfamily Tillandsioideae and have entire (spineless) leaves. Mostly epiphytic, some of the larger species can survive as terrestrials in their native habitat. They grow mostly in the humid forests and can be found from sea level to mountain areas of 3000 m or more. Some species are found in Florida, but most are found in the highlands of Colombia and southwards down to western Brazil.

The inflorescence is long-lasting and polystichous (with branches radiating from the axis). The bracts are usually vivid in colour and range from yellow to brilliant orange and red. Petals are usually white or yellow and, when in flower, guzmanias glow with flamboyant colour.

The genus has undergone numerous name changes. Synonyms include *Caraguata*, *Sodiroa*, *Schlumbergeria*, *Massangea* and *Devillea*.

The absence of spines make these plants desirable for growers who dislike prickly plants and need colour to enhance their potted plant collections. Many species have glossy green leaves, some are pencilled with delicate brown or red lines towards the base of the plant. Others are crossbanded or etched with bizarre markings. Most are small to medium-sized, making them ideal for greenhouse culture, but some are very large indeed. Most of these large species come from the high Andes, and while beautifully marked, they are rather difficult to grow at low elevations, as well as taking up considerable space.

Guzmanias are jungle plants from hot tropical areas and are cold sensitive and need care in winter to prevent them from rotting.

They need to be snugly potted (that is, in a pot just a little larger than the root area, allowing for about one year's growth, before potting on to the next size pot and fresh compost). Use a potting mix that will retain a little moisture, but allow all excess water to drain away freely. This is especially necessary in winter so that the plants do not suffer from 'cold, wet feet' overnight. A cymbidium orchid mix is usually suitable if you don't wish to mix your own compost. The following mixture in a well-crocked pot will grow most guzmanias: two parts of fine pine chips, two parts of sphagnum peat and a half part of pea-sized charcoal. A slow-release fertiliser such as bone meal is also of benefit.

During the summer the plants need to be watered about twice per week with misting on alternate days. Take care to do this in the late afternoon or evening and not during the heat of the day, otherwise leaf burn may occur. Ease up on the programme in winter, spraying about every one to two weeks early in the day and misting on the odd sunny morning to keep plants from dehydrating. Do not water in the evening during cold periods as 'cold burn' can occur during the night. Generally speaking, care must be taken when watering during winter as the plants are in their resting period.

Do not fertilise guzmanias until they are in rapid growth during the warmer months. Try to rush them during cold weather and they go into a quick demise. Most losses occur in early spring when we get impatient with their return to normal growing. Given time they soon respond to the warmer days and reward us with their bright floral display.

Guzmania Species

Keeping in mind the comments made earlier, the following are some guzmanias that can be grown well in cultivation in the British Isles given a minimum temperature of 60°F (15°C). Some species can tolerate lower temperatures for short periods of time, but tip water out of the rosettes in winter to prevent scorching.

If you search around, some of the following species will be available.

Guzmania berteroniana lights up like candles on river banks or on trees in the forests of Panama, Jamaica, the Dominican Republic and Puerto Rico from 500 to 1000 m altitude. It has glossy green leaves in a medium-sized rosette and the infloresence rises up like a glowing red poker.

Guzmania bipartita is rare in cultivation. An imposing plant from the humid forests of the highlands of Ecuador and northern Peru. Golden-green leaves reach up to 3¼ ft (1 m) tall from which a rich, glossy red cone-like inflorescence arises on a single or double spike. Each spike can have from 30 to 70 bright yellow flowers.

Guzmania conifera comes from the Andes mountains of Ecuador and Peru at an altitude of about 1000 m. A large, bright-green species, reaching to 3¼ ft (1 m) in height. The scape reaches to about the height of the leaves, where bright red floral bracts, tipped with yellow, form a dense, cone-like inflorescence.

Guzmania danielii is found high in the trees in the rainforests of Colombia between 1500 and 1800 m altitude. It is a large, imposing, reddish plant with a cylindrical flower head of red bracts and yellow flowers.

Guzmania dissitiflora is found in the hot, humid, dark forests of Costa Rica, Panama and Colombia, between 75 and 1500 m altitude. A small plant with narrow, light green, pencil striped, recurving leaves and a lax spike of red bracts and yellow flowers.

Guzmania donnell-smithii comes from the humid forests of Costa Rica at an elevation of 300 to 650 m. It is a medium-sized plant with light-green leaves marked on the undersides with red. The stiff, bright red inflorescence ends in a cluster of bright yellow flowers and boat-shaped, red bracts.

Guzmania erythrolepis is found in the rainforests of Cuba, Jamaica and Puerto Rico between 550 and 1000 m altitude. It is a medium-sized rosette and there are two forms. One has soft, leathery leaves of apple-green and bracts of pale coral-pink. The second form has darker leaves tinged with purple and the bracts are orange-red. The flower head is a dense cone and the flowers are yellow.

Guzmania gloriosa (Plate 20) has been found in the dry, sandy regions of Ecuador at 1800 m as well as in the dense forests of Colombia up to 2750 m. This is one of the giants of the family. It has medium green leaves marked at the base with red stripes. The tall, thick spike is green at the base, then golden-yellow and the top is scarlet with bright yellow flowers in clusters from the axils of the bracts.

Guzmania lindenii grows both as a terrestrial and as an epiphyte in its native central Peru, in humid forests at about 2300 m elevation. A large species with light green leaves marked with transverse wavy lines. As with many of the beautifully marked foliage types, the inflorescence is not startling, but it is still attractive, whether in flower or not.

Guzmania lingulata (Plate 19). The various varieties of this are found through the islands of the West Indies, Central America and down into Brazil. It is found from sea level to 1000 m altitude and was one of the first bromeliads to be described. Mez gave it the name we know it by today. *Guzmania lingulata* is relatively easy to grow in medium light in a greenhouse or conservatory. It is a green plant with up to 30 leaves and has brilliant red bracts and creamy-yellow flowers.

Varieties of *Guzmania lingulata* are:

Guzmania lingulata var. *minor* is the smallest of the varieties. The outer bracts of the inflorescence are orange-red.

Guzmania lingulata var. *splendens*. This is a larger plant with leaves marked with red-purple stripes. The spike terminates with a funnel-shaped, purple-red head of flowers. The centre bracts are tipped with white.

Guzmania lingulata var. *cardinalis*. The outer bracts are bright scarlet and spreading. Larger and more brilliant than var. *lingulata*.

Guzmania lingulata var. *flammea*. This is a small green plant. The outer bracts of the few-flowered inflorescence are erect and bright scarlet. The bracts are tipped with white.

Guzmania melinonis is a medium-sized plant with a cylindrical inflorescence of red or orange bracts and bright yellow flowers. One of the easiest to grow but its spike is not long-lasting. (See *Guzmania remyi* for a description of the plant which most growers have wrongly labelled as *Guzmania melinonis*.)

Guzmania monostachya has green leaves, forming a dense rosette, and its habitat covers the greatest geographical range of the genus. It is found from Florida to Brazil and from sea level to 1800 m altitude. It grows under a variety of conditions, but usually as an epiphyte in humid conditions. The inflorescence is tricoloured. The cylindrical spike is green at first, then the lower half takes on red lines and the upper part vivid red with snowy white petals.

Guzmania monostachya var. alba has wholly green bracts of which the colour lasts about one month.

Guzmania monostachya var. variegata is native to Florida and has green and white, longitudinally striped leaves.

Guzmania musaica has beautiful leaves marked dark green, brown and purple in mosaic-like patterns. It is found in Panama and Colombia, from sea level to over 1000 m altitude, growing in mangrove swamps as well as on trees. It must have good aeration as nothing will kill it as fast as still, cold air in winter. The globular spike on a 1 ft (30 cm) scape is flesh coloured and changes to scarlet. Waxy white flowers peep from the bullet-shaped inflorescence. It is sometimes hard to propagate, but well worth every effort to grow it.

Guzmania nicaraguensis is found on trees in the forests of Mexico and Central America from 750 to 1000 m elevation. A medium-sized plant with thin pencil lines on the green leaves. The short spike has a red cone with yellow flowers.

Guzmania patula comes from the hot, dark forests of Costa Rica, Venezuela, Colombia and Brazil at elevations of 1375 to 1800 m. Variable in size from small to medium. The brownish leaves are red lined and the slender scape is erect. It has a somewhat cylindrical spike with white or greenish petals.

Guzmania remyi is restricted to the western slopes of the Andes, in central and northern Ecuador and non-flowering plants can be mistaken for *Guzmania melinonis*, mentioned earlier. *Guzmania remyi* has a cylindrical inflorescence, usually longer than *Guzmania melinonis*, with pink or rose-purple bracts, mostly tipped with white. The flowers are white.

Guzmania sanguinea grows as an epiphyte in the dense, wet forests of Costa Rica, Colombia, Venezuela, Trinidad, Tobago and Ecuador at elevations between 275 and 2000 m. The plants often cover their host tree. There are two forms of this unusual guzmania. The small form, var. *brevipedicellata*, has leaves only about 8 in (20 cm) long while var. *sanguinea* has leaves 19 in (48 cm) or more. The large rosette of greenleaves tinted with red in the early stages, gradually becomes spotted with violet-red, changing later to blood-red. The colour varies in individual plants and their centres intensify as flowering approaches. The flowers hidden in the centres are not showy, but the leaves and central bracts make up for that. Usually only one offset appears in the centre of the plant and great care must be taken if you wish to remove it. Most growers wait for the old leaves to die off and then repot the plant lower in the pot. The variety *brevipedicellata* usually produces two offsets in the centre of the plant.

Guzmania squarrosa comes from Ecuador, Colombia, Venezuela, Peru and Guiana at elevations of 1000 to 2450 m. Usually epiphytic, it is found growing low in trees alongside streams. The colourful, bronzy leaves, whose brown scales give it its name, grow to nearly 3¼ ft (1 m) high. The brilliant red inflorescence is on a short scape and soon passes. The flowers are white.

Guzmania vittata is a medium-sized plant that comes from the hot, humid forests of Brazil, Colombia and Peru where it grows at about 175 m. It needs care in winter to keep it looking good. More than ten narrow, curled leaves, strongly crossbanded with deep green or purple on the undersides, form a funnel-type rosette. The slender, tall green spike terminates in ovate form of one or several spikes of pale green bracts, spotted with purple. The petals are white.

Guzmania wittmackii comes from the dense rainforests of the Colombian Andes. It is a large plant with a candelabra-type of inflorescence with richly coloured bracts varying in colour from lilac to rose and scarlet. The flowers are white. Although an epiphyte, it can be grown in pots as a large specimen where space allows.

Guzmania zahnii is native to dark forests of the mountains of Panama and Costa Rica at elevations of about 1400 m. It is a small plant with slender, glossy green leaves pencilled with reddish-brown or crimson. The central leaves take on reddish tones and become coppery-red in good light. The tall spike has orange-red bracts and yellow flowers.

Guzmania Hybrids

There are a number of unnamed hybrids to be found in collections, but in recent years the following have become available and can be found if you are willing to hunt around. Information may be obtained from various bromeliad societies and specialist nurseries listed in Appendices 1 and 2.

Guzmania 'Fantasia' is a cross between *Guzmania zahnii* and *Guzmania donnell-smithii*. Of medium size with attractive pencilled, soft green leaves and a tall spike with boat-shaped red bracts and yellow branchlets of flowers.

Guzmania 'Orangeade' is a large, yellow-green plant with a glowing orange-red inflorescence that lasts in colour for many months.

CHAPTER 11

NEOREGELIA

Figure 10   *Neoregelia carolinae* var. *tricolor*

The 'Blushing Hearts' of the Bromeliad family well deserve their popularity. Easy to grow and adapting to many conditions, they are most rewarding for house, greenhouse or conservatory.

Most neoregelias are medium-sized and grow in a compact, flat rosette. In their natural habitat they vary in size from 2 in (5 cm) across to a diameter which can approach 5 ft (1.5 m). The flowers are in a compound head nestled in the heart of the plant; these are usually blue or white, and die quickly, but the flush of colour in the often brilliant foliage of this genus remains for many months. A distinguishing feature of many species is a heart that turns red, vivid-rose or purple when blooming time approaches. The leaves may be plain green, silvery-green, maroon, banded, spotted, striped or marbled and may be soft or firm in texture. They are largely natives of eastern Brazil, but a few species are found in Amazonia and in eastern Colombia and Peru.

Epiphytic bromeliads differ somewhat from other plants in that their root systems function primarily to anchor them to rocks, tree trunks or branches of trees. In their natural state their roots are exposed to the air, so they must have good drainage when grown in pots.

Neoregelias in nature develop stronger root systems than when confined in pots. This is particularly manifested when rich decaying matter is available. They are not deep rooted and when growing naturally, send out their roots laterally in search of food. They love to get their roots under rocks, where it is always moist and cool.

Neoregelias obtain most of their nutrition from the soup in their cups. Bird droppings, leaves and other decaying matter all contribute to feed the plant. Their cups should never be allowed to dry out, although in extremely cold weather, they should be emptied out so the water does not freeze. Only in the terrestrial bromeliads which have no tanks or cups to hold water are strong root systems developed for their sustenance.

Containers

No offset or 'pup' should be potted up until it has roots. When taken from the parent plant it should be put into a box in damp peat moss or sand. This way it will grow roots faster than being in a pot on its own, where it can easily miss being watered.

When it is evident from examination that roots are present, the plant can be transferred to an appropriately sized pot or container. It can then be repotted at intervals to larger containers as the plant develops in size.

The leaf bases should not be set any deeper than the top of the compost. Contact with leaf axils can encourage rot. If the plant does not have a good root system, a few stones around the base will hold it upright until it has grown enough roots to stabilise itself. Remove the stones before offsets appear, otherwise growth will be inhibited.

The pot size depends on the plant. If underpotted it can become top heavy and fall over. You are confronted with a never-ending job of putting the plant back in place and topping up with soil again. Apart from this, a big plant in a small pot looks absurd, although compact plants are often grown to perfection in small containers. When the roots start to emerge from the drainage holes in the pot, it is a sure sign that the plant is overdue for a larger container. Without waiting for this to happen, it is easy to pull the plant out to see if its roots have taken up all the medium, but only after the plant has been in the pot for at least six months.

Some growers like to pot a plant in a big container from the beginning. They consider it saves work, as the plant stays in the same pot for its whole life. It is considered, however, that if this practice is followed, watering would have to be watched, as the compost could sour without the root growth to utilise the extra soil.

When neoregelias are used in permanent displays they may need replanting from time to time to keep the display looking attractive. The site might be unsuitable and the plant does not do well, or leaf burn from the cold or the heat may occur. Some grow too large and hide the other neoregelias. It takes only a few unsightly plants to mar the effect of a landscaped display. Where plant leaves lie parallel with the ground and rest on it, they are susceptible to rot and die. The grower is constantly removing unsightly leaves. Also, ground-hugging leaves harbour pests and it is difficult to spray under them.

The average sized neoregelias with the rosette form are the best to use in a permanent display. They should be grown at ground level, so that their blooming hearts can be seen. The back of the bed should be raised so that the back plantings are not hidden by the front plants, and their pots tilted to the viewer so that their vivid beauty can be appreciated.

Miniature neoregelias should be grown hard. Shallow containers and bright light will maintain their colour. Hanging baskets bring out the best in the miniatures. When grown in too much soil they lose their appeal; the leaves grow long and lush with no colour. The difference between a hard-grown miniature and a lush-grown plant of the same species or clone is so great that it is hard to believe they came from the same clump. Water sparingly, give them bright light and not too deep a growing medium.

Mixture

Neoregelias can be grown successfully in many materials and there are as many potting mixtures as there are growers. One suggested mixture uses equal quantities of fine pine bark, coarse sand or river gravel and peat-based compost. If you have charcoal, it is an excellent addition as it helps to keep the mixture pure, and improves drainage.

Charcoal has become expensive to use but products such as perlite will act as a substitute. The latter however does not possess the same purifying qualities.

Some growers like to use sphagnum moss in their mix, but this is a matter of personal preference. Besides being very dear, it becomes a soggy mass if it is watered too much. On the other hand, it dries out completely if watering is postponed and is difficult to rewet. However, it is useful in seed trays to root offsets. Moist sand is also successful for this.

Light and Temperature

Sunlight is one of the most important aspects to consider when growing neoregelias. The coloration of leaves and the growth are determined to a great extent by the light factor. In their natural state, these plants grow under diverse conditions. Some with tough leathery leaves can take full sun, others with softer foliage dwell in dappled light under trees and usually the green-leaved forms are found in shade. Neoregelias will vary in size and colour, depending where they are grown. When the light is too strong the plant becomes bleached and loses its rich, luxuriant appearance.

Examine your plants and if they have soft, glossy leaves, protect them against extremes of light, heat and cold. Even if they do not show the effects of burn, the hot dry days of early summer will bleach the colour and they lose that vibrant rich look which is so special about the genus *Neoregelia*. Most will grow well in the house as long as the air is not too dry.

To prevent scorching in summer, shading will be required to protect the plants. If sunlight becomes intense and temperatures soar during summer months, 70 per cent shading provided by either paints or fabric may be necessary.

A minimum temperature of 45°F (7°C) will be sufficient in winter as long as the plants remain dry. However, some of the softer-leaved species may show cold burns on the ends of their leaves if temperatures drop down low at night. It should be noted that in most genera the variegated bromeliads are the most prone to suffer from extremes of temperature.

Water and Humidity

Neoregelias are quite tolerant of dry conditions. With water in their cups they are able to withstand periods of drought, but will fare better with a regular pattern of watering.

Pot-grown plants should be kept moist. If the drainage is good, rot and base-rot will be minimised. In the rosette form, the water runs off the ends of the leaves and unrestricted roots will travel out to take up this moisture. In a container-grown plant the roots cannot spread out to the leaf drip line. After watering ensure that all the compost is moist and not just the top layer. Uneven watering can cause the roots to grow towards the top of the pot and inhibit the growth of the plant.

Water sparingly in winter but increase this to twice a week in summer, with daily misting of the leaves. Avoid the heat of the day and water in the late afternoons or early evenings during summer, and early mornings during winter. Humidity will also determine how much water is required. The tank in the centre of genus *Neoregelia* is a characteristic, developed over many generations to sustain the plant, not only providing water but also nutrients.

Humidity is important if we are to grow neoregelias well. Bromeliads absorb moisture through their leaves and this is why they enjoy frequent mistings. On hot, dry days when humidity is low, these plants can burn easily, but in high temperatures they will not burn if the humidity is high. Misting frequently on dry days helps to lessen the likelihood of burning. Shading the house or conservatory will substantially reduce the chances of scorching.

Fertilising

At the 1985 Bromeliad Conference in Brisbane an excellent lecture was given by John Wilkins on the effects of fertilisers on neoregelias. The following are excerpts from John's speech, printed with his permission. Enthusiasts in the British Isles will also find the results of great interest.

The application of fertilisers to bromeliads has always been a controversial subject. This is not surprising when one considers the nutrient requirements of plants, the varied environments in which they are grown and the differing objectives of growers. Additionally, recommendations often tend to generalise, sometimes causing problems with specific genera or under special growing conditions. This is particularly true of the element nitrogen (N). Certainly it is difficult to find agreement in published literature, journals, or even in commercial catalogues.

There seems to be a majority judgement in the United States that the genus *Neoregelia* should not be fertilised until after flowering. However opinions differ and local experienced growers have successfully applied foliar fertilisers to neoregelias or put slow-release or other fertilisers in the potting mixture and still have achieved prize winning plants.

It must be realised that nature does not always produce optimum plants and man can generally improve on 'natural' conditions to achieve superior plants. It was to help resolve some of these conflicting theories that I commenced a fertiliser experiment in 1982 of the genus.

The plants were all grown outdoors in the same area, in pots sunk into pine bark under a covering of 50 per cent shade cloth. The plants were examined at approximately six monthly intervals and repotted into larger pots as necessary up to a maximum of 6 in (15 cm) pots. The observations were designed to check growth, form, colour and offset production and specifically to determine the extent to which the element nitrogen (N) was friend or foe to these factors.

In August 1982, eleven near-identical offsets were originally potted in 4 in (10 cm) pots using a mixture comprising: one part sieved pine bark; one part peanut shell; one part peat moss; one part charcoal.

John went on to detail ten different fertilisers used on ten of the plants with one receiving no fertiliser. After trial over two to three years John's conclusions are:

In drawing conclusions from one limited trial, one must be careful not to be too dogmatic. Environments under which plants are grown differ, growers' cultivation methods vary, and from separate observations I am convinced that light plays a more significant role in achieving good colour in neoregelias than fertiliser practices. Nevertheless, I have concluded to my own satisfaction that in relation to genus *Neoregelia*:

1. A fertiliser (not slow release) added to the potting medium gives best combined growth, form, colour and offset production.
2. The formulae of the fertiliser should be in the approximate proportions — 15% nitrogen (N); 5% phosphate (P); 15% potassium (K). The nitrogen should be derived from urea or ammonium phosphate and the potassium preferably from potassium sulphate.
3. The amount used is not critical but should be about one level teaspoon to a 5 in (13 cm) pot, mixed with the potting medium.
4. pH is not critical but the potting medium should be on the acid side; that is, lower than 6.0.
5. There appears to be little benefit in fertilising neoregelias after flowering to induce additional offsets. I suspect that the triggering mechanism for offset production is already fixed by flowering time.

Finally, . . . properly used in balance with other elements, nitrogen can indeed be a friend and not a foe.

Some growers use fertilisers, others do not. Some prefer to foliar feed and others mix fertiliser in with the potting mixture. Each has his or her own favourite, be it slow-release, foliar or 'normal' type. In general be very sparing with the use of fertilisers. Foliar feeding, for example, should be used at only half the strength (or less) recommended on the container. Also keep in mind that neoregelias rest in the winter, their dormant period, so do not try to force them into new growth by foliar or other feeding. Wait until spring. In other words use fertilisers only during the warmer months.

Bromeliads grow more slowly than a lot of other cultivated plants, so their reaction to adverse conditions takes longer to show. Sometimes it is too late to remedy the situation since it can take some months before a plant will show if conditions are harmful to its welfare. The most eloquent sign is dying at the leaf ends. This could be due to heat or cold, underwatering or overwatering. Among the first intimations that something is wrong, is when a plant turns a vivid hue, usually out of season. The brilliant centre will topple over, a victim of rot, mostly caused by overwatering in winter, but there are many other reasons for rot in a plant. If not getting enough light, the new growth will be weak and spindly and there will be no colour in the leaves.

Plants need grooming regularly. Unsightly and dead leaves should be removed periodically. When growth starts, they should not be restricted around their bases. If too tightly potted, water cannot drain easily from their axils, and if held too long a foul smell develops and rot can set in. Growing in their natural state, frequent and heavy showers clean out the stagnant water. When grooming the plants, do not remove so many leaves that the soft white portion of the stem is exposed. This soft tissue is vulnerable to fungus attack. It is best to cut the leaves off near the base if they are yellow or dead. Where leaf burn has occurred on the ends of the leaves, cut the burn back, trimming to the same shape as the unburnt leaves. Dust can be easily removed with a dry cloth or tissue.

All neoregelias need good air circulation, but cold draughts can adversely affect them. In their natural habitats, they are subject to wind, sometimes very strong winds, and apparently thrive on these conditions, obtaining various nutrients from leaves and debris blown into their centres. Winds carry nitrogen, carbon dioxide and trace elements. Decaying matter also adds food.

Stoloniferous neoregelias are suitable for planting in bromeliad trees, either those which are natural or those constructed from sections of cork bark. Plants for display should have their roots wrapped in sphagnum moss and tied up with nylon fishing line. Securely fasten them in the crotches or on the branches, as it will take from one to two years before the plants can grow roots and anchor themselves to the host tree. As the stolons grow, use the largest types of staples to secure these in place.

The harder the conditions, the better the colour, but there is no need to go to such extremes that the plants are starved for water and their leaves shrivel inwards. When grown as epiphytes the plants should be watered daily or misted.

Neoregelia 'Fireball' is a magnificent specimen on a stump or a branch, as is *Neoregelia chlorosticta* 'Rubra'. The old favourite, 'the fingernail plant' or *Neoregelia spectabilis*, is superb when grown in the crotch of a display tree in bright light. The true beauty of the plant lies under the leaves, where the deep rose-pink is accentuated by soft grey barring and can only be seen to its best advantage high up above eye level. *Neoregelia scandens* produces exceptionally long stolons. It is not noted for its bright colour; its leaves are grey, but it should make a good subject for tree culture. Another neoregelia with long thin wiry stolons – is *N. hoehneana*. The ampullacea 'forms' are suitable as tree dwellers but they need bright light to keep their ampule shape and markings. They are capable of tolerating almost full sun.

The following neoregelias are all worthy of general cultivation.

Neoregelia ampullacea is a miniature plant measuring about 1–1¾ in (2–4 cm) in diameter and 5 in (12 cm) in height. The tubular leaves are green, flecked and crossbanded with maroon. The flowers are deep in the tube and have blue margins and white centres. This species is ideal for hanging baskets and bromeliad trees, because of its stoloniferous habit.

Neoregelia carcharodon is a very large, robust species with stiff, leathery leaves about 2 ft (60 cm) long and 2¾ in (7 cm) wide, grey-green in colour, spotted purple above and heavily banded underneath, with very prominent purple spines and red tips. It has white flowers edged with lavender. This species is very hardy and will stand full sun.

Neoregelia carolinae is the most widely cultivated member of the genus. The medium green leaves 1 ft (30 cm) long and 1¼ in (3 cm) wide form a compact rosette. The colour of the centre when flowering is variable, from cerise to a deep crimson. It has lavender flowers deep in the cup.

Neoregelia carolinae var. tricolor is a variegated form with green and cream stripes. When blooming approaches, the whole plant becomes suffused with pink, and the inner leaves around the cup turn a vivid crimson, which lasts for many months. It also has lavender flowers.

Neoregelia compacta is an erect, compact rosette. The leaves are green and about 8–10 in (20–25 cm) long. The inner leaves turn a fiery red at flowering, and the petals are also red. The offsets are produced on long stolons.

Neoregelia concentrica has broad, leathery leaves which form a large, compact rosette about 2 ft (60 cm) in diameter. They are green, heavily blotched with maroon or purple, with black spines and red tips. The reverse side is heavily banded with silver-grey. When flowering, the inner leaves turn a deep purple. The flowers are blue.

Neoregelia cruenta is another large species. The leaves, which are about 2ft (60 cm) long and 3 in (7.5 cm) wide, are a light straw colour. It has conspicuous red spines and red tips. The underside has heavy, maroon barring. At flowering the inner leaves turn bright red. It has blue flowers sunk deep in the cup.

Neoregelia fosteriana is an upright, dense rosette about 16–24 in (40–60 cm) in diameter. The leaves are a dark burgundy, lightly dusted with grey, and burgundy-red tips. It has blue flowers.

Neoregelia marmorata (Plate 24) is a medium-sized plant with pale green leaves about 1 ft (30 cm) long and 2 in (5 cm) wide. The leaves are heavily marbled on both sides with irregular blotches of reddish-brown and tipped with vivid red. The petals are lavender.

Neoregelia 'Painted Desert' (Plate 25) is a beautiful Hummel hybrid, medium to large in size. The red-tipped green leaves form an attractive rosette, are heavily blotched with red which intensifies in bright light. The flowers are blue and deep in the cup.

Neoregelia pauciflora is a miniature tubular plant 5–6 in (12–15 cm) high. It has leaves of olive-green, heavily blotched with dark purple and grey banding on the undersides. The flowers are white and sunk deep in the tube. The offsets are produced on long, thin, wiry stolons making this plant ideal for hanging baskets and bromeliad trees.

Neoregelia punctatissima is a small, tubular plant with green leaves, white crossbanded on the upper sides and brown spotted underneath. The inflorescence rises on a short scape, the flowers are white.

Neoregelia spectabilis is commonly known as the 'painted fingernail plant'. This species has been an old favourite for many years. A medium-sized, open rosette, with leaves about 1 ft (30 cm) long and 2 in (5 cm) wide, of olive-green colour above and grey bands underneath and bright red tips. It has violet-coloured flowers. When grown in bright light the plant assumes a 'pinky' tone, especially on the undersides of the leaves.

Neoregelia zonata is an upright, robust plant 8–12 in (20–30 cm) high. The leaves are olive-green, heavily blotched and banded with dark red on both sides, but more prominent on the undersides. They have brown spines and are tipped with red. It has pale blue flowers deep in the cup. This plant is also ideal for hanging baskets.

CHAPTER 12

NIDULARIUM

Figure 11   *Nidularium*

This is a small genus of about 30 known species, all native to eastern Brazil, where they grow on the ground or on the lower limbs of trees in shadowy, humid rainforests.

They are compact, medium to large plants mostly with shiny, soft foliage and are finely toothed. They vary in colour from lime-green to black-purple and can be spotted, striped or just plain green. A rosette of shortened inner leaves in the heart forms before flowering and most species project their inflorescences above the open rosette of leaves. A few have a stalk about 6 in (15 cm) tall. The egg-like flowers nestle in the bracts, giving them their nickname of 'birdnest bromeliads', and the name *Nidularium* is taken from the Latin 'nidus' meaning nest. The inner cluster of colour is confined to this collarette of leaves which turn either bright red, orange, yellow, cerise or maroon. The small flowers are either white, blue or orange-red but are not as spectacular as some of the other bromeliads, e.g. *Aechmea* or *Billbergia*.

Nidulariums are sometimes confused with neoregelias but they have softer spines and larger bracts separating the flowers. Most species project their inflorescences above the open rosette of leaves and not down in the cup like neoregelias.

Compared to neoregelias, they generally play second best but a well-grown nidularium in full colour can hold its own against anything. As they are a small genus of plants they are not grown as much as neoregelias. In addition, since they prefer a lower light than neoregelias, they should be grown more like guzmanias. Keep the soil moist but well-drained.

Be careful with them so far as location is concerned, as the soft foliage can burn in hot summer sun. When taking pups off the plants, don't take them too early, let them get to at least one-third the size of the parent.

Keep your nidulariums neat and tidy by taking off dead or yellow leaves — you can remove the hard-to-remove ones by splitting them down the centre and pulling one half sideways to the right and the other to the left. If some of the leaves have brown tips you can trim them with sharp scissors, but be sure you trim them the same shape as the others; nothing looks as bad as leaves hacked off raggedly.

Containers

Most nidulariums are terrestrial bromeliads so they grow well in containers and develop fibrous roots which absorb nutrients just as well as other plants.

Most pots are either made of plastic or terracotta with drainage holes in the bottom or sides. Terracotta (clay) pots are porous and provide good aeration, but dry out very quickly and are heavy if you want to transport them to shows or displays. Being heavy, they also give good support to large plants. On the other hand, the lighter plastic containers restrict aeration but conserve the moisture of the potting soil. Ceramic pots are very decorative but make sure that they have drainage holes, otherwise you can very easily overwater. As a result, not only will accumulated salts build up in the potting medium, but the plant can rot.

Hanging baskets can be made of plain plastic or wire. The plastic type don't need any lining and last for years. The wire ones must be lined with something, such as:

1. a layer of live sphagnum moss which needs to be replaced periodically.
2. coconut fibre — which is quite expensive, but can now be bought as ready-made liners.
3. black plastic — which does not look the best and only lasts a couple of seasons.
4. a matting liner that you can buy at garden centres.

Terrariums or fish tanks are a good way of growing some of the small nidulariums as they like the moist atmosphere, but open them daily so that they get plenty of fresh air.

When you pot the pups (offsets) don't overpot (use too large a pot) as they grow better when they are rather rootbound. They do best in about 4 in (10 cm) pots until they outgrow this size. Full-grown nidulariums don't need any more than a 6 in (15 cm) pot. Growing these plants in containers for indoor decoration is a fascinating interest for bromeliad growers, especially for those who have little space. They are popular in the foyer, entrance hall and office of many business premises and will produce adequate results with the minimum of attention if they have a humid atmosphere, filtered light and even temperature. Misting three or four times a week is beneficial.

Mixture

To grow nidulariums successfully the potting mixture must be friable, porous and slightly acid. Admittedly there must be some moisture-holding capacity but it must not become sodden. You can use orchid compost which is generally quite expensive, so to make it go further add some charcoal (to keep the mixture sweet). To improve the drainage add coarse river sand (the coarser the better) or vermiculite.

Use a good quality compost. Tree fern fibre, sphagnum peat, bark chips and leaf mould will add acidity. Add a slow-release fertiliser, like bone meal for food. Of course you don't have to include all these substances but trial and error will tell which potting medium will work best for the environment that you have created in your greenhouse or conservatory. Always use moist compost as there is less chance of damaging tender new roots when it is damp. To test the moisture content take a handful of compost and squeeze as hard as you can, when you open your hand the soil should fall freely and not stay in a soggy ball.

Don't pot the crown of the plant too deeply as the moisture around the crown could rot the plant. If it is not too firm in the pot try holding it with a wooden or wire stake. Be sure the wire is plastic coated as copper or galvanised wire will injure the plant.

One nidularium that does best in a poor compost is *Nidularium innocentii* var. *lineatum* as too-rich a compost will cause it to become green and lose a lot of its attractive white stripes.

Light

Nidulariums will tolerate the lowest light conditions of all bromeliads, but don't grow them in too dark a spot because the leaves will become too strappy. They can be grown under slatted or mesh benches in the greenhouse.

Nidulariums adapt quite well to household conditions as long as they get bright light, but not direct sunlight as this will burn their soft foliage. This is especially so with species having maroon-coloured leaves, for example *Nidularium billbergioides* var. *rubra*. Light is the most important factor affecting indoor plant growth.

Bromeliads can be grown under artificial lighting. Fluorescent tubes and mercury vapour lamps are the best. The nearer you can get to natural lighting the more success you will have.

Water and Humidity

Winter watering of nidulariums should be kept to a minimum, allowing the compost to become barely moist. Winter wet will cause the plants to rot. If you grow your plants inside your house, where the heating dries the air be sure to mist about every second day so that you keep up the humidity. A simple handspray is all that you need.

Summer time is much easier, just bear in mind the great importance of keeping the centre of the plant full of clear water. Nidulariums that are grown in pots should remain moist but not soggy. Too much water even in summer could rot plants. It is better to water the pot thoroughly two or three times a week, rather than just water lightly each day. In the latter case the water will not go down to the roots where it counts. Flush out the tank (centre cup) of each plant now and again to rid it of accumulated salts. Use rainwater whenever possible. Don't water in the heat of the day as the soft and sometimes glossy foliage of nidulariums could burn. In summer it is better to water very early in the morning, or better still, after the main heat of the day has gone. Not that you have them in direct sunlight, but the water tends to get rather warm on the foliage because of the heat. The presence of dry patches on otherwise glossy foliage is an indication of heat or water burn.

Temperature and Air Circulation

Nidulariums need a minimum temperature of 54°F (12°C). They require good air circulation at all times so don't crowd them in your bromeliad 'house'. If you grow them indoors, place them in an airy position but avoid cold draughts.

Remember that they are tropical plants whose natural habitats are humid forests in Brazil. Where conditions allow, it is beneficial to put them out to enjoy some fresh air during summer, but be sure to bring them in before the sun can get to them as their foliage will burn.

Fertilising

Fertilisers can be used, but only during the warmer months when the plants are growing. They respond well to liquid foliar feeding but be sure to use it only at half the strength recommended on the container. Only use it about four times at monthly intervals, otherwise the plants will grow too lush and too green; in other words they will lose their attractive colours and stripes.

When repotting, small amounts of slow-release fertilisers can be added to the potting mixture, such as hoof and horn or bone meal. Never use fast-release fertilisers high in nitrogen as this will cause lush sappy growth or scorched roots.

Small Growth

Nidularium billbergioides var. flavum has a small rosette of long, narrow leaves, the spines are inconspicuous and it is one of a few species that have their flower heads on 6 in (15 cm) stalks. The bracts are orange with white petals.

Nidularium billbergioides var. citrinum (Plate 26) also has long, narrow leaves with a bright yellow inflorescence on a 6 in (15 cm) stalk.

Nidularium billbergioides var. rubra has maroon-black leaves with a maroon-black inflorescence on a 6 in (15 cm) stalk.

Nidularium billbergioides variegata has darker green leaves with yellow margins and orange bracts on a 6 in (15 cm) stalk.

Nidularium burchellii is another small form with lustreless leaves, green above, purple below. The inflorescence rises a little from the rosette, has white flowers later turning to orange seed pods lasting for months. It is a species that likes to climb and is good on a bromeliad tree.

Medium Growth

Nidularium billbergioides (Plate 27) has dark green leaves 20 in (50 cm) long and 1¼ in (3 cm) wide forming an upright rosette. The beautiful flower spike appears on the end of a tall 6 in (15 cm) stalk. The bracts are orange and the flower petals white.

Nidularium fulgens (Plate 28) hsa shiny, lime-green, serrated leaves mottled with darker green flecks. Dark blue flowers with white edges in bright cerise bracts that turn pale lavender. There is also a form with orange bracts.

Nidularium innocentii has wide leaves with a midrib, purple, glossy underneath and dull dark green and maroon on top (with a rusty red inner rosette). There is also a smaller form *innocentii* var. *purpurea* which has almost black leaves.

Nidularium innocentii var. wittmackianum (Plate 29) is nearly the same as var. *innocentii* but has all-green leaves with white flowers.

Nidularium innocentii var. lineatum has pale green leaves striped white, sometimes with more stripes than green. The centre has a most attractive red inflorescence with white flowers.

Nidularium innocentii var. striatum has green foliage with white lines in the middle of the leaves. Both var. *lineatum* and var. *striatum* are temperamental in winter. Don't feed them too much as the leaves will lose some of their stripes and turn towards green.

Nidularium regelioides has broad, rich green, shiny leaves mottled with dark green flecks. The inner rosette is a rich rose colour with dark orange flowers.

Nidularium scheremetiewii has bright green, serrated leaves about 12 in (30 cm) long and 1 in (2.5 cm) wide. The inner rosette is bright red with violet flowers.

Nidularium rutilans is nearly the same as *regelioides* but has no flecks. The inner rosette is a dark rose colour.

Nidularium procerum var. kermesianum is a medium-sized version of *Nidularium procerum* (see below).

Large Growth

Nidularium procerum is a large, robust plant with long, leathery leaves which are green, tinged with rust or copper. The showy red bract has orange-red flowers.

CHAPTER 13

TILLANDSIA

Figure 12   *Tillandsia dianthoidea*

Tillandsias are members of the subfamily Tillandsioideae and of all the bromeliad family comprise the largest number of species and cover the widest range of territory. Identified species presently number in excess of 500 and new varieties are being discovered each year. They are found throughout South America from Argentina to Venezuela and Colombia; in Central America from Panama to Mexico and the West Indies.

They are perhaps the most fascinating group in the entire plant kingdom, and are regarded by many as the aristocrats of the bromeliad world, with their great variation in shape, size, leaf formation and general adaptability in their native habitat.

Nearly all tillandsias are epiphytes or 'air-plants', and take in moisture and nutrients through their leaves. They have a relatively small root system, sufficient to secure them to their support. Some are terrestrial while others are saxicolous. They vary in size from 2½ in (6 cm) to about 13 ft (4 m) in height and may be found in all sorts of locations in the wild, from sea level to high altitudes, growing in sand, on rocks, cliff faces, tree trunks and branches, and on desert cacti.

Those that grow in the hot, dry regions can have greyish, green or reddish foliage, and are covered with a silvery scale that resembles 'star dust'. These are commonly referred to as the 'silver' or 'grey' tillandsias. The soft, green-leaf species live high in tree tops in the cool or humid rainforests or semi-open woods.

The miniatures are the species *Tillandsia bryoides* and *Tillandsia tricholepis* and are found in Argentina, Bolivia and Peru at elevations from 700 to 3000 m. *Tillandsia tectorum* grows on rocks in Ecuador and Peru from 1000 to 3000 m. At the other end of the scale, the giant *Tillandsia grandis*, which grows to 13 ft (4 m) when in bloom, is found from Mexico to Honduras where it also grows on rocks.

The magnificent *Tillandsia wagneriana*, which is a soft, green-leaved species that could at first be mistaken for a vriesea, is found only in the hot, humid jungle in the Amazonian regions of Peru. *Tillandsia benthamiana*, *Tillandsia macdougallii* and *Tillandsia ponderosa* are a few of those which dwell in the high cloud forests. These examples serve to illustrate the amazing versatility of the genus.

In cultivation, tillandsias have adapted well, allowing that there is a limit to what growers can do to produce ideal conditions.

The grey tillandsias are easy to grow in partial or full sun. They also require good air circulation at all times.

A minimum winter temperature of 50°F (10°C) is adequate for most species, although some, such as *Tillandsia ionantha*, can tolerate temperatures of 40°F (5°C). In summer, during the afternoons after the heat of the day has gone, the plants can be sprayed over with water using a hose pipe or taken and dipped in a bath of water.

The high altitude and green leaf species require entirely different light and temperature conditions. Their soft leaves will burn if exposed to direct sunlight and need filtered light at all times. They need a minimum winter temperature of 60°F (15°C). The watering and misting programme for the warmer months is the same as outlined above, but in winter the plants need water infrequently, keeping the compost just moist. They can be misted occasionally in the early part of the day.

The green-leaved species respond well to being grown in pots. Terracotta or plastic pots are quite suitable. The growing mix must be coarse and well-drained; avoid 'wet feet' at all costs. Pine bark chips or an open orchid mix have proved successful compost components.

As most species are epiphytic the majority in cultivation are mounted on pieces of suitable material which is normally suspended so that plants receive plenty of air circulation.

Mounting tillandsias, particularly the grey-leaved types, may be done in a number of different ways, usually on cork bark, small pieces of driftwood, or tree branches cut to size. With cork bark or material of similar surface composition a very effective method is to glue the plant on lightly with a silicone adhesive, taking care that any root growth that may be evident is not buried under the glue. Determine beforehand the manner and position in which you want the plant to be secured; it may be necessary to cut a groove or recess into the material to obtain the best effect.

Avoid applying the glue directly under the base of the plant if possible; it is best to apply it to one side near the base. Remember, this may be a temporary arrangement; as the plant grows it will send down its roots which in most cases will fasten securely to the material. Once the plant is placed in position leave it to dry.

Fixing plants to driftwood, bark or light branches is best done with fine, plastic-covered wire; this provides complete freedom for root development and is strong enough to secure larger and heavier plants which may break away from glue. Do not use bare wire as contact with metals such as copper or zinc can have detrimental, even fatal, results.

As most tillandsias produce offsets or 'pups' they may be left undisturbed to grow on into clumps, which has strong appeal to some hobbyists. With some species it is desirable to break up the clump eventually by removing old, dead growth to maintain the clean appearance of the colony.

The alternative approach is to remove the offsets when they reach about one-third the size of the parent and mount them separately to build up individual groups. Some species have offsets which are easily removed, such as *Tillandsia tricolor* and *Tillandsia secunda*; in fact any offset that emerges from the base of the parent plant can be removed without much trouble. However, the fleshy-stemmed types which produce their pups from between the leaf axils are difficult to remove. Great care is necessary to remove these without damaging the young plants, which may not survive if the base is broken or cut. Species in this category include *Tillandsia argentea, Tillandsia didisticha, Tillandsia magnusiana, Tillandsia meridionalis* and *Tillandsia vernicosa*.

If the parent has produced multiple offsets it is better to sacrifice it and ensure the safe removal of the young. Start at the bottom of the parent and remove all the leaves, moving upwards. When the bases of the pups are reached it is fairly simple to cut or lever them gently from the main stem. In most cases there will be root growth established in the stem of the parent, which should be carefully cut. Leave the young plants for at least a week to enable their bases to dry and harden off. Avoid contact with water during this period.

If the parent plant has only produced one offset, it is better not to remove it as others may emerge at a later date. This may not occur if the parent is damaged for the sake of one offset.

Opinions are evenly divided on the need for fertilising; certainly in their natural environment they can exist on very little nutrient. The purely epiphytic species subsist almost entirely by the absorption of gases such as carbon dioxide and ammonia, and dissolved organic material from the atmosphere. It can be argued that in the covered environment of cultivation, where the natural conditions are somewhat modified, liquid feeding can certainly do no harm. Perhaps it is a situation for the individual to experiment and observe the results. It must be emphasised, however, that the fertiliser must be used sparingly. With foliar feeding the strength must be half (or less) that recommended by the manufacturers.

The following list describes a few of the popular and easy-to-grow species in cultivation. They may be sold loose or be already mounted on a base.

Tillandsia aeranthos is a small plant 4 in (10 cm) high, with about 20 fine, narrow green leaves, covered both sides with greyish scales, which form a neat rosette. Striking when in flower, bracts are bright reddish-purple, petals violet-blue. A beautiful species but variable in size.

Tillandsia albertiana is a small, dainty plant 10–12 in (25–30 cm) high with few leaves, fine and tapering to a point, covered with grey scales. It has a prominent, single, scarlet red flower resembling a three-leaved clover.

Tillandsia argentea is a dainty plant 1½ in (3 cm) across resembling a pin cushion, with many fine, needle-like leaves 3 in (7 cm) long, silver-grey in colour. The inflorescence is rose with mauve petals.

Tillandsia bergeri is one of the easiest to grow and multiplies well, quickly forming clumps. The grey-green leaves are 3 in (7 cm) long, the scape about the length of the leaves, and the flower head is compact with flared blue and white petals.

Tillandsia brachycaulos forms a tight rosette 8 in (20 cm) across of light green leaves 4 in (10 cm) long. Leaves turn scarlet red at flowering. Numerous purple flowers rise progressively from the centre of the rosette. There are several forms of this plant, all suited to pot culture.

Tillandsia bulbosa is an extremely variable plant in size and coloration. The bulbous base is dusted with silver scale, the light green leaves twist and curl about, ranging from 6–10 in (15–25 cm) in length. Its short scape is red with dark blue petals.

Tillandsia capitata is a very stylish plant, ideal for pot culture. It forms an open rosette up to 20 in (50 cm) across, with numerous firm, slightly curving greenish leaves. A stout spike emerges to support the open inflorescence. Many bright mauve flowers rise progressively from the open head. There is a green and red form of this plant.

Tillandsia caput-medusae is a bulbous plant measuring 1½–2½ in (4–6 cm) across, with about 15 leaves, wide at the base, tapering to a point, curved and twisted, heavily covered with silver-grey scale. The scape is up to 8 in (20 cm) long with several spikes of red or yellow, and dark blue petals.

Tillandsia cyanea is a very beautiful and well-known tillandsia, particularly when in flower. Mostly grown in pots it comprises a tight rosette, many fine, grass-like leaves to 14 in (35 cm) long. The inflorescence has a flat, fan-shaped head from which striking dark blue flowers emerge.

Tillandsia fasciculata (Plate 30). There are some ten forms of this variable species, ranging from 10–40 in (25–100 cm) high, with stiff, narrow, grey-green leaves. The flower stalk is erect, prominent and branched, with bracts red, yellow or green, petals violet. Can be potted or mounted.

Tillandsia filifolia (Plate 31). A beautiful and delicate, fine-leaved plant in the shape of a dense rosette. The leaves are grey-green and about 3–5 in (7–12 cm) long. The inflorescence is branched and the petals are lavender.

Tillandsia flabellata is found in cloud forests in its native habitat and does well in cultivation. Suitable for pot culture, it is rosette-shaped with long, soft-green or reddish leaves about 20 in (50 cm) across. Up to eight bright red, slender bracts with blue petals emerge from the centre.

Tillandsia gardneri is a classic tillandsia that likes dry conditions. It forms a compact rosette with numerous silvery-white, soft leaves, velvety in texture. Bracts are light green to pale pink, clustered, with bright red petals. Somewhat variable in size.

Tillandsia ionantha is a group of various small forms that grow in clumps, adaptable species found in both dry and moist regions. Small, tight rosette with leaves averaging 2 in (5 cm) long covered in silver grey scales. Prior to flowering leaves turn brilliant red. Flowers are violet.

Tillandsia jucunda is a small, silver-green plant with narrow leaves 3½–7 in (9–18 cm) long. The inflorescence may be simple or branched and has rose bracts. The petals are yellow and fragrant.

Tillandsia juncea is a variable species with at least three forms. The stiff, upright leaves, to 20 in (50 cm) high, are grey-green with silver scales on the underside. An erect, branched scape with bright red bracts and purple flowers.

Tillandsia leiboldiana is a small plant 6–10 in (15–25 cm) in diameter with thin leaves forming a cup-like rosette. The foliage is usually speckled with maroon at the base. The spike has red bracts and the flowers are mauve.

Tillandsia lindenii likes moist conditions. It forms an open rosette with many narrow, green leaves to 16 in (40 cm) long, with fine reddish parallel lines. The flower spike is elongated, flat, up to 6 in (15 cm) long and 2 in (5 cm) wide, flowers purplish-blue. Very attractive in bloom and ideal for pot culture.

Tillandsia magnusiana (Plate 33) is a charming species with a bulbous base, with many fine silver-grey leaves branching out to form a compact shape, 5 in (12 cm) high and 8 in (20 cm) across, densely covered with silver scales. The scape barely protrudes from the foliage from which two long, violet petals appear.

Tillandsia mauryana (Plate 32) is an attractive, rosette-shaped species, with numerous grey-scaled leaves arching out from the centre, about 5 in (12 cm) across and 4 in (10 cm) high. A compact inflorescence of 6 to 8 spikes, from which tubular, dark green petals emerge.

Tillandsia meridionalis is an attractive plant suited to sunny, semi-dry locations; 6 in (15 cm) across and 4 in (10 cm) high, with short, stout, silvery-grey leaves forming a compact rosette, well covered with silver scales. The scape is slender, slightly arched, bracts bright pink with small white petals.

Tillandsia pruinosa (Plate 35) is a plant with a bulb-like base 1¼ in (3 cm) across and up to 5 in (12 cm) high, leaves round in appearance that twist and curl, heavily covered with silvery scales. It has a short scape with pink bracts and purple petals.

Tillandsia pueblensis is a slender, upright plant 6–8 in (15–20 cm) high with a somewhat bulbous base, heavily covered with grey scales. Inflorescence is about 4 in (10 cm) long, the bracts are pink, petals violet. A very durable species.

Tillandsia punctulata enjoys a cool, damp and shady situation. Numerous narrow, green leaves, wider and darker at the base, arch out. It is 16 in (40 cm) across with a 12 in (30 cm) high spike. Bracts are bright red, petals white at the base, otherwise blackish-blue. An appealing species that does well in pots.

Tillandsia setacea is variable in size. The green leaves, resembling pine needles, can be 4–12 in (10–30 cm) long and turn a reddish colour in sunlight. It forms a dense rosette that grows in clumps containing many individual plants. It has a pink stalk and purple flowers which group at the apex.

Tillandsia streptophylla (Plate 36) is sometimes referred to as 'curly locks' because of the tapering leaves curling up into ringlets. Variable in size with prominent bulb-shaped base, leaves green or grey covered with silver scales. The inflorescence comprises 10–15 mostly horizontal spikes coloured delicate pink, petals light blue. A very distinctive species.

Tillandsia stricta is a charming plant adaptable to both wet and dry conditions. A small, compact rosette with many green, tapered leaves covered lightly with silvery scales. The inflorescence is somewhat pendulous with pink or red bracts and blue petals that gradually turn red.

Tillandsia usneoides is commonly known as Spanish Moss. This species is quite different from all other tillandsias. It has thin leaves 1–2 in (2–5 cm) long that grow at intervals along a slender stem covered with silver scales. The tiny green flowers are on short stalks, appear in the axils of the leaves, and are fragrant. The stem may grow many metres long making it a very striking and different plant to hang from trees or cork bark. It is an unusual species.

Tillandsia xerographica (Plate 34) can grow to 2ft (60 cm) in diameter and 3 ft (90 cm) high when in flower. The silvery-grey leaves are wide at the base and taper to a point making an attractive rosette. The inflorescence is densely branched on a green stem. The bracts are red, the floral bracts are yellow-green, and the petals are purple. This plant must be watered very sparingly, especially during winter.

CHAPTER 14

VRIESEA

Figure 13   *Vriesia corcovadensis*

Vrieseas in their native habitat extend from Central Mexico in the north to as far south as Argentina, although they are mainly concentrated in Brazil. They are found in forests from sea level to several thousand metres altitude. The larger species are found growing as terrestrials on exposed hillsides, whilst the smaller, usually soft-leaved types are found in warm humid forests. Most are epiphytes, with a general preference for trees where they receive dappled light and adequate air circulation in conjunction with warmth and humidity.

Generally, vrieseas are medium-sized plants. However, they can vary in size from about 6 in (15 cm) to approximately 5 ft (1.5 m) in height and diameter. They have smooth-edged, green leaves which are usually soft and flexible, although a few species have foliage that is relatively firm and less pliable. The leaves come in shades of green from very light to extremely dark, almost black. They can be spotted, blotched or barred.

The spike of the inflorescence has green, yellow or white flowers. It is mostly erect, but some species have pendent or semi-pendent types. The brilliantly coloured bracts are green, purple, red or yellow, and retain their colour for many months.

Vrieseas adapt well to cultivation, providing certain guidelines are observed when growing this lovely genus. Following these will reward the grower with healthy plants, large flower spikes and plenty of offsets.

Containers

Most pots are made of plastic or terracotta with drainage holes in the bottom. Either type is suitable but care should be taken if using terracotta pots as they will dry out very quickly. Plastic pots are both lightweight and sturdy, but black plastic should be avoided in very hot conditions as this colour tends to absorb and hold heat for longer periods than other colours. Whilst this may not cause problems in direct sun it can result in 'cooking' any new roots, with dire results.

Some species, such as *Vriesea patula*, *Vriesea espinosae* and *Vriesea olmosana*, should be grown epiphytically in similar fashion to grey tillandsias, mounted on cork or other suitable material. Nearly all other vrieseas available in cultivation can be grown successfully as terrestrials.

Compost

As vrieseas are mainly epiphytes, good drainage is essential. These plants require an open mixture which drains freely and dries out quickly. Avoid any material that decomposes quickly as this can affect good drainage and thereby damage delicate root growth. It is suggested that potting mixtures should be composed of equal parts of pine bark chips, coarse sand or perlite, leaf mould or sphagnum moss.

All of the above materials are used by various growers and each grower has his or her favourite 'combination'; all are successful to various degrees and only trial and error will provide you with the best combination for your particular growing conditions.

Light

Vrieseas grow under various light conditions but moderate light would be the best for most species available in cultivation. This, together with good air circulation, is necessary to grow these plants successfully. It is believed that air movement with vrieseas cannot be over-emphasised as the secret in growing healthy plants. Most will require shading in summer if grown in greenhouses or conservatories.

Water and Humidity

The first question people ask is, how often do vrieseas need water? This can be answered in most cases by observing the different leaf types of the various species. Soft-leaved plants come in the main from dense forest areas where they receive frequent rain and should be watered approximately two to three times per week in the summer months and kept just moist during winter. The harder-leaved plants will also survive under these conditions provided good drainage is present. However, the latter will be happier with less frequent watering, particularly during colder months, and kept dry if the temperature drops below 45°F (7°C).

During summer, watering or misting should be carried out after the heat of the day has gone, i.e. late afternoon or early evening. If it is done in the morning make sure it is early so that water on the leaves has dried off before the heat of the day hits them and causes leaf burn.

The level of humidity surrounding your plants is important and care should be taken to maintain, if possible, a relative humidity of about 60 per cent. This can be achieved on hot days by misting the floor of the greenhouse or conservatory so as to keep the floor moist but the plant leaves dry. Water on the leaves on hot days can cause burning and unsightly marks on the foliage. Overhead misting systems will create humidity but care should be taken to follow the guidelines given above.

Temperature

Many species are tolerant of low temperatures during the winter months. Several experiments in the USA have shown vrieseas to be 'freeze stalwarts', particularly those coming from Brazil. Most can withstand sudden drops in temperature far below the normal accepted minimum of 45°F (7°C).

Fertilising

The particular method of fertilising the plants is a matter of personal choice. Slow-release fertiliser may be added to the potting mixture, or spread on top making sure the granules do not fall into the leaf axils or touch any part of the plant.

Liquid feeds are probably the easiest to use and any orchid or indoor plant type is suitable for bromeliads. Care should be taken, however, to use only half the recommended dosage levels. Soluble fertiliser should be used during the warmer months only, whilst the plants are growing, and applied at monthly intervals. Foliage vrieseas, such as *Vriesea hierogly-phica*, require feeding regularly or growth will be slow; likewise green vrieseas rely on fertiliser for the size and colour of their flower spikes.

The following plants are recommended to the beginner. Reference to Appendices 1 and 2 will help in locating sources of supply.

Vriesea bituminosa prefers diffused light and moist locations. Medium-sized plant 24–30 in (60–75 cm) high and 18–24 in (45–60 cm) across when in flower. The leaves are broad, medium green, lightly marked with lavender and a brownish-red blotch at their rounded tips. Scape prominent, with greenish-yellow bracts and pale pink petals.

Vriesea carinata is a small plant with soft, light green leaves, and forms a small rosette up to 10 in (25 cm) across. The inflorescence has been compared to crab or lobster claws, bracts red at the base, changing to yellow and green at the tips, with yellow flowers emerging in sequence.

Vriesea ensiformis is a variable, small to medium grower, with soft, light green leaves with a lavender hue. The flat, sword shaped flower spike has dark red bracts with yellow petals. There are several forms of this plant with some variations in colour.

Vriesea erythrodactylon is a small plant to 14 in (40 cm) across and 18 in (45 cm) high in spike, with soft green leaves turning brownish-blue at the base. Scape erect, widening at the top, bracts pointing upwards, green at base, red tips and yellow petals.

Vriesea fenestralis is a tall, graceful plant up to 3¼ ft (1 m) high in flower. The leaves are a combination of greenish-yellow stripes all over with variable patches of dark greenish-purple. The inflorescence is tall with branched green bracts and yellowish petals. A very attractive foliage plant.

Vriesea fosteriana (Plate 38) is a large attractive foliage plant. The broad leaves up to 3¼ ft (1 m) long form a dense compact rosette, the foliage being medium green with uneven bands of red-brown to maroon coloration on both sides. The flower spike is prominent with two opposed rows of green bracts with yellow flowers.

Vriesea gigantea, a large plant, is favoured for its foliage of blue-green leaves blotched both sides with yellow-green checked patterns. Inflorescence over 3¼ ft (1 m) high with spikes branching upwards, green with yellow green petals.

Vriesea heterostachys is a variable plant in size and colour. The leaves can be green or have a reddish tinge and the size can vary from 8–18 in (20–45 cm) in diameter. The inflorescence, on a green stem, tends to lean outwards when it reaches the level of the leaves. The tall floral bracts are bright orange with a lacquer-like stem.

Vriesea hieroglyphica. Known as 'King of the Bromeliads', this is a majestic species. The large rosette stands over 3¼ ft (1 m) high. Numerous broad, bright green, glossy leaves up to 5 ft (1.5 m) across are prominently marked with crossbanding of dark green to blackish-purple. Flower spike up to 2 ft (60 cm) long with branched, yellowish-green bracts and yellow petals.

Vriesea platynema (Plate 37) has broad, leathery leaves that form a rosette which can reach about 3 ft (90 cm) diameter. The foliage is bluish-green with faint wavy lines on the upper sides of the leaves and a soft purple underneath. The simple inflorescence rises on an erect scape. The bracts are purple or red and the petals green or yellow.

Vriesea platynema var. variegata is a medium-sized species with beautiful leaf markings, reddish-blue on undersides, greenish-yellow stripes on upper sides with plum-coloured tips. Spike prominent, bracts purple, petals light green or yellow.

Vriesea psittacina (Plate 39) is a small to medium-sized plant with soft, light green leaves that sometimes have violet shading towards the sheath. The beautiful feather-like inflorescence has overlapping flower bracts which are multi-coloured, red, yellow and green. The petals are yellow with green spotting.

Vriesea saundersii is a small plant with numerous leaves, 14 in (40 cm) across, forming a dense rosette, dull grey-green with irregular reddish-brown spots. Grown in good light it has a faint rosy hue. Infloresence about 10 in (25 cm) long, bracts greenish-yellow, petals yellow.

Vriesea scalaris (Plate 41) is a dainty miniature with a small rosette 8 in (20 cm) in diameter, soft, light green leaves, distinctive pendulous spike about 6 in (15 cm) long, with flowers branching off left to right, bracts yellow, flowers green.

Vriesea splendens is cultivated by commercial nurseries and is frequently seen in retail outlets. Commonly known as flaming sword, it is a very impressive plant of medium size, with soft green leaves prominently banded with purplish-black markings. Inflorescence 18 in (45 cm) high, with sword-shaped spike of bright red or orange, flowers are yellow.

Vriesea zamorensis is a large plant with numerous soft, dark green leaves about 18 in (45 cm) long and 2 in (5 cm) wide, forming an open rosette 12 in (30 cm) high. the inflorescence can reach a height of 20 in (50 cm), with up to 12 branched spikes of rich orange-yellow. A very attractive species.

CHAPTER 15

LESSER KNOWN GENERA

This chapter deals with some of the more unusual genera and a few of the species pertaining to each genus, which for one reason or another are not seen as much in cultivation as those discussed in earlier chapters.

They are of interest to those growers who seek to enlarge their collections with a wider spectrum of bromeliads covering some less common types, broadening their cultural knowledge in the process. Most opportunities for acquiring plants occur by meeting fellow enthusiasts and occasionally at specialist nurseries. Appendices 1 and 2 list sources.

Short descriptions and condensed cultural notes are given in each case and this information, brief as it is, should provide a basis for further exploration of the bromeliad world.

Abromeitiella

This small genus is native to areas of south Bolivia and north-western Argentina, where it grows on rocks in hot, dry conditions forming vast cushions of tiny, grey-green, stiff rosettes. At a glance these plants are not unlike tiny dyckias. The two most frequently seen in cultivation are *Abromeitiella brevifolia* from south Bolivia and north-western Argentina, and *Abromeitiella lorentziana* from north-western Argentina.

Usually grown by succulent fanciers, they require similar culture. In other words, bright light and a gritty, well-drained mixture in pots.

Acanthostachys

Acanthostachys strobilacea is the only species in this genus, and is native to central and south-eastern Brazil, Paraguay and northern Argentina. Growing high in trees in tropical rainforests or clinging to granite peaks at moderate to high elevations, its leaves are long, dull green to reddish-brown depending on light intensity and are whip-like in appearance, with serrated edges. An attractive long-lasting inflorescence develops at maturity, resembling a tine pineapple with orange-red bracts and yellow petals. The species is self-fertile and when ripe the berries can be planted for propagation.

Because of its form, *Acanthostachys strobilacea* is very attractive for hanging pot or basket culture, grown in bright, filtered light. It grows well in lightly shaded conditions. An open, well drained cymbidium orchid mixture is very suitable as a growing medium. Do not cover more than the plant's roots when repotting. It needs good air circulation around the leaf base to avoid rotting.

Androlepis
A large, showy plant of rosette form with green foliage bronzing in good light. The only known species of this genus is **Androlepis skinneri**, native to Central America where it grows on rocks or as an epiphyte. Resembling a robust aechmea, this interesting bromeliad produces a tall, semi-cylindrical, semi-branched inflorescence with light yellow petals.

Androlepis skinneri makes an attractive specimen. It requires warm winter conditions and bright, filtered light. The plant should be watered very sparingly during the coldest periods. An open, well-drained mixture is essential.

Araeococcus
This genus is found in Costa Rica, Central America, Guiana, West Indies and Amazonian Brazil. Usually epiphytic but sometimes saxicolous, these plants require warm winters and are not the easiest plants to cultivate.

Occasionally, **Araeococcus flagellifolius** is found in cultivation. It prefers a very coarse compost with its roots only just covered and grown in bright, filtered light. It requires extra care during winter. Unless your conditions are similar to that which this plant enjoys in nature you are unlikely to succeed with this one.

Araeococcus flagellifolius has an attractive inflorescence with red stem and many small, pink flowers followed by deep blue berries. The quaint, long, bronze, whip-like leaves, coupled with the delightful inflorescence, makes one attempt to grow this plant under often unsuitable conditions.

Bromelia
This genus is native to Central America, Venezuela, Panama, Guiana, the West Indies, Colombia, Peru, Ecuador, Paraguay, Uruguay, Bolivia and throughout tropical America, but the greatest number of species are indigenous to Brazil. Bromelia are found in a variety of locations—in dunes by the sea, dry open forest, sandy fields, on the edge of rainforests, on creek or river banks, in thorny scrubland and areas of higher elevation.

They are saxicolous or terrestrial, rarely epiphytic, of rosette form, usually with green foliage, though sometimes the leaves are reddish-brown. All very spiny, most quite large, these plants when not in flower resemble the genus *Ananas*. Difficult to handle because of their thorns which have a habit of alternately curving up then down, *Bromelia* aren't widely cultivated. However, at the height of summer their flaming hearts and glorious inflorescences with large, often lavender petals, are a sight to behold.

Bromelia need full sun, large containers and lots of space. They offset on stolons and soon make large clumps. If you have a roomy area full of sun, these plants will reward you with their fiery hearts and obvious inflorescence, and for a moment you forget their treacherous thorns.

Bromelia balansae (Plate 40), *Bromelia antiacantha* and *Bromelia pinguin* are all large plants, hardly met with in cultivation.

Canistrum

Only a small number are in cultivation. Perhaps this is because some grow into quite large plants, occupying more than their share of space in the average greenhouse. They derive their name from the basket-like form of their bracts and the general arrangement of their flowers. Canistrum leaves have a serrated edge but could hardly be termed 'spiny': possibly comparable to nidulariums.

Indigenous to eastern Brazil, their distribution extends from the southern state of Santa Catarina to as far north as Pernambuco. However, most of the species and varieties are from the central-eastern region with some extending to the mountains of Minas Gerais.

These plants enjoy an average to warm 55–86°F (13°C–30°C) temperature all year round in their native habitat and generally require winter warmth.

Most canistrums are epiphytic so they require an open mixture; for example, a cymbidium orchid mixture would be suitable. Plants growing terrestrially in habitat have generally fallen from their lofty perches and nestle their roots in the layers of leaf litter below. Do not overpot, but the larger forms if allowed to cluster would require a pot of shrub tub proportions eventually.

Medium to bright, filtered light suits them well with the plain green foliage forms tolerating the medium level.

All canistrums come from areas of high humidity. Mist frequently in dry weather. During the warm months they can cope with regular watering. During winter give them enough to keep the compost just moist.

Because of the size of most of the species in cultivation, fertilising is hardly necessary and they will grow and bloom if provided with a good, open potting medium.

Canistrum lindenii and its many varieties grow and flower in lightly shaded conditions. The very beautiful *Canistrum lindenii* var. *lindenii albo-marginata* and *lindenii variegata*, with their white-on-green variegations, must be given the care of any other rare tropical foliage plant. Their very foliage makes them more susceptible to cold than the plain green varieties. A little care and the unblemished beauty of the foliage more than repays.

Canistrum aurantiacum from Pernambuco in hot, north-eastern Brazil, found at almost sea level as an epiphyte and also as a terrestrial, requires winter warmth in filtered, medium to bright light.

Canistrum cyathiforme has a long scape and cup-like bract arrangement.

From an area of winter warmth in the state of Bahia in north-eastern Brazil comes *Canistrum fosterianum* with a tubular, grey-green, dark blotched form quite different from the usual large green rosettes. Its inflorescence on a long stem is a rose shade, looking almost incongruous on the beautiful but strange plant. The flower petals are white. *Canistrum fosterianum* var. *pardinum* is smaller than the species, with leaves of apple-green tipped with black and splashes of black at the leaf base. This plant is an upright rosette. Again the strange inflorescence on the long stem, with the bracts this time a definite orange shade.

Perhaps too large for most gardens, but certainly stunning with large red bracts and contrasting white flower petals, *Canistrum 'Leopardinum'* is a hybrid using *Canistrum ingratum* and *Canistrum lindenii* var. *roseum* as parents.

Catopsis

The genus *Catopsis* belongs to the subfamily Tillandsioideae and, like all other members, has no spines. The recorded catopsis species are chiefly found in south Florida, Central America, The Greater Antilles and the northern region of South America. *Catopsis berteroniana* and *Catopsis sessiflora* have been found as far south as Santa Catarina in southern Brazil.

Quaint rather than highly coloured, these usually small bromeliads have soft, waxy leaves frequently coated with white powder, especially on the leaf reverse. Their inflorescences are of elongated or branched form, the petals white. They are usually epiphytic, sometimes saxicolous. Consequently they can be mounted, or grown in a coarse, well-drained compost. A medium to warm, 55–86°F (13°–30°C), year-round temperature is enjoyed in their homelands. Grow in bright, filtered light ranging to full tropical sunlight. Mist daily in dry periods to maintain a reasonable level of humidity. Some catopsis found more frequently in cultivation are *Catopsis hahnii* from southern Mexico and areas of Central America, *Catopsis morreniana* from similar regions, *Catopsis mexicana* native to Mexico, *Catopsis berteroniana*, *Catopsis sessiliflora* with possibly the widest habitat distribution, and *Catopsis floribunda* from south Florida through the West Indies to Venezuela.

As a novelty plant, catopsis will fill the need.

Deuterocohnia

One of the more primitive of the bromeliad family, deuterocohnias are small to large perennial plants which form a curious ring arrangement in habitat. Native to Peru, Chile, Bolivia, Brazil, Paraguay and Argentina, they are saxicolous or terrestrial and are an interesting addition to a succulent collection. Of rosette form, their leaves may be serrated to densely spined. Slow growing, they eventually flower with a tall inflorescence of small, white petals. These plants are interesting rather than beautiful.

The two usually found in collections are *Deuterocohnia schreiteri*, a silver-leaved form from north-western Argentina growing high on rock outcrops, and *Deuterocohnia longipetala*, collected on dry rocky slopes of northern Peru to north-western Argentina.

Of easy culture in a terrestrial mixture and well-crocked container, grow in a bright area with little water.

Fascicularia

Another small, rugged genus from Chile. In habitat these plants are saxicolous or terrestrial, growing in very exposed areas by the sea. Fasciculares can be grown in full sunlight and survive sudden cold spells most bromeliads dislike. They make excellent plants for succulent enthusiasts. Blooming in autumn, their hearts turn fiery red and produce many blue-petalled flowers.

Two species usually found in cultivation are *Fascicularia bicolor* and *Fascicularia pitcairniifolia*. Both have compact clusters of many narrow, grey-green leaves with serrated edges. Both offset freely, soon forming attractive colonies.

Fosterella

More quaint than colourful, these small terrestrial plants have a geographic range from Mexico to Argentina. Their leaves can be smooth or spiny. In habitat they grow often in rocky areas of semi-shade.

Only a small number are cultivated to any extent. Possibly the best known is *Fosterella penduliflora* with soft, grey-green leaves in a flat rosette. The inflorescence is branched with many small, white, bell-shaped flowers.

Fosterella villosula with bi-coloured leaves of grey-green above and wine red reverse, has a more attractive foliage although the flowers are rather similar to *penduliflora* and also white in colour. Other fosterellas worth cultivating are *Fosterella schidosperma*, *Fosterella micrantha* and *Fosterella weddelliana*.

102

These plants are of easy culture in semi-shade. Use a well-drained terrestrial mixture of sandy loam and added peat moss with a well-crocked pot. A sprinkling of slow-release fertiliser can give them an added boost.

Hohenbergia

This medium-to-large, clumping genus is like the bigger robust aechmeas in appearance and is of similar culture. They are found growing as epiphytes, saxicolous on rocky outcrops and as terrestrials in dunes near the sea. Hohenbergias are found in Venezuela, the West Indies and Brazil with the north-eastern state of Bahia providing the largest number of species.

The best known of the species and probably the most colourful is *Hohenbergia stellata* with its star-like arrangement of flowers with vivid red bracts and deep blue petals. The inflorescence retains its colour for many months. This species is found in the West Indies, Venezuela and Brazil and grows in trees or as a terrestrial.

The less colourful *Hohenbergia ridleyi* produces a tall spike with lavender petals. Some other species are *Hohenbergia portoricensis*, *Hohenbergia attenuata* and *Hohenbergia penduliflora*.

Hohenbergias are robust in appearance but require winter warmth to do well and medium to bright light. Moderate water and humidity and a good open growing medium. Don't over-pot but increase pot size in proportion to plant growth.

Neoglaziovia

A monotypic genus from the hot, dry, arid region of north-eastern Brazil where it grows in shallow rocky soil in open scrubland. The leaves are long, narrow and somewhat rounded with whip-like tips. Its fibre is used for weaving in its homeland and the stoloniferous plants can grow quite tall. The inflorescence has pink bracts with purple petals turning darker with age. Grow as a succulent in a well-crocked mixture, in bright light. Water moderately to sparingly, keeping in mind that its natural habitat is hot and humid, but with low rainfall.

There are two forms, *Neoglaziovia variegata* and *Neoglaziovia variegata* var. *concolor*. The former is occasionally seen in succulent collections. Its leaves with broad white crossbands can be quite appealing. The var. *concolor* form is not banded and is covered in dense, white scurf on both sides of its leaves.

Ochagavia

This small genus, native to Chile and the off-shore island of Juan Fernandes, is another of the more primitive of the bromeliad family. Growing saxicolous or terrestrial at low to high altitudes in sunny locations in nature, these rugged plants present no problem in cultivation. Of clustering habit, with spiny, narrow leaves and rosette form, they adapt well to succulent-type culture.

Possibly the best known is *Ochagavia carnea* with its medium size and attractive silver leaves. The floral bracts are a deep rose-pink and of ball-shaped formation supporting lavender flowers with pronounced yellow stamens.

Grow in a succulent-type mixture (coarse sand, fine gravel, or similar, with some leaf mould added for nourishment) in sun or part sun in a well-crocked container. Under these conditions *Ochagavia carnea* will flourish and reward you with its stunning inflorescence.

Orthophytum

All orthophytums are native to areas of Minas Gerais, Espirito Santo, Bahia and Paraiba in central to northern-eastern Brazil. They all have white flowers. These curious plants are found growing in rock crevices and high on granite cliff faces above streams, frequently at high altitudes, with constant seepage often providing dampness to their roots.

In habitat, cool to medium temperatures of 50–75°F (10–24°C) are experienced all year and although they will tolerate higher or lower temperature conditions, they will not tolerate low light.

Orthophytums are easy to grow as succulents and are an interesting genus for pot culture in bright, filtered light to full sun. Add a liberal amount of coarse grit to the potting medium to provide the requisite good drainage. Low to moderate water is required for these plants with a preference for the potting mixture to be almost dry before watering again. The almost fleshy leaves of many of this genus help them through any prolonged dry periods.

Possibly the most desired orthophytum in cultivation is *Orthophytum navioides* with long, narrow, green, arching leaves which turn crimson as flowering approaches. Other widely grown species are *Orthophytum saxicola* and its green variety *viridis*, *Orthophytum vagans*, of trailing habit and green leaves turning crimson in full sun, and *Orthophytum foliosum* with its spiralling habit at flowering.

Pitcairnia

The genus *Pitcairnia* is second only to the genus *Tillandsia* in its abundance. With recorded species and varieties approaching 300 its distribution extends from Central America to as far south as Argentina, with the largest concentration in Peru, Colombia and Brazil.

In habitat, pitcairnias are usually saxicolous or terrestrial, occasionally epiphytic. A number lose their leaves during the dormant period of winter, regaining them after flowering in spring. These forms require an area of bright warmth and overhead cover in cultivation. Too much water during the winter rest period, which is dry in their homeland, can cause them to rot.

Pitcairnia heterophylla is the best known of the deciduous forms which actually produces two forms of foliage on the same plant. It has a bulbous base with this area in particular heavily spined. Glorious red flowers, occasionally white on some varieties, cover *Pitcairnia heterophylla* in spring. Succulent culture is recommended for this plant. It is native to southern Mexico, Panama, Venezuela and northern Peru.

Pitcairnia andreana is of loose rosette form and is often seen in cultivation, usually in a hanging pot or basket. Its attractive orange and yellow petals make it most desirable. This plant needs winter warmth and is native to Colombia.

Pitcairnia atrorubens is another species often seen in subtropical and tropical gardens. Its eye-catching inflorescence of dark red bracts with white petals is very showy. It is native to Panama, Costa Rica and Mexico.

Pitcairnia tabuliformis is a much desired species producing a flat, outspread rosette of leaves and long, yellow petals; it makes a suitable pot specimen. This is another one requiring winter protection and a dormant period before its spring flowering. *Pitcairnia tabuliformis* is found in the state of Cheapas in southern Mexico.

Pitcairnia flammea is usually trouble free and easy to grow in cultivation. It comes from the slippery, water covered granite rocks in the Organ Mountains region of Rio de Janeiro state in south-eastern Brazil. The plant has at least seven varieties. Many growers like to have a pot of the red and the white flowered forms, both very attractive in spring.

Pitcairnia spicata from Martinique in the Windward Islands, growing high on mountain slopes, is another species gaining popularity in cultivation, requiring just a little care in winter. The plant has long, red petals, and its grey-green foliage is rather squat and tapering.

Pitcairnia xanthocalyx, with its tall inflorescence of pale yellow petals and bright green foliage, is of easy culture and is native to Central Mexico.

Only a few of the many Pitcairnias identified are in cultivation. Most present no problem in cultivation and make excellent pot specimens. The evergreen forms require moist, well-drained conditions. Their foliage is usually green and grass-like.

However, during spring into summer their attractive flower spikes of white, cream, orange, red, yellow and sometimes a combination of several colours, can create great interest.

Portea

Indigenous to the coastal area of Brazil, the distribution of this genus extends from the states of Paraiba and Pernambuco in the north, to Rio de Janeiro in the central coastal region. In habitat, porteas are saxicolous or terrestrial, and occasionally epiphytic.

They are medium to large plants of spreading or upright rosette form, resembling the larger stately species of the genus *Aechmea*. Their long-lasting inflorescences are said to be comparable with any of the more decorative bromeliad species. Usually their foliage is green; however *Portea kermesiana* can be blotched wine red on the upper sides of the leaves and wine red on the reverse, or in high light intensity the entire plant may turn this colour. It requires winter warmth in cultivation.

The species or varieties usually found in cultivation are *Portea petropolitana* and its variety *extensa*. The name 'petropolitana' is from the mountain area of Petropolis in Rio de Janeiro state, the location from which the first specimen was collected. A variety with an inflorescence of even more beauty and more intense colour is *Portea petropolitana* var. *noettigii*.

Portea lepantha from far northern coastal Brazil forms a large rosette about 5 ft (1.5 m) across with strap-shaped leaves. The flowers are widely branched and orange in colour.

For the novice, *Portea petropolitana* and its varieties are far easier to grow and flower and make excellent pot specimens. However, realising their size at maturity, grow in a bright, warm place in a large greenhouse or conservatory.

All plants of this genus need bright light and warm conditions in a well-drained growing medium.

Puya

Puyas have spiny leaves, in some species very much so. The foliage can be green, or grey to white in those which are heavily dusted with absorption scales. This frosted appearance enhances their beauty considerably.

In regions of marked seasons, puyas establish and flower regularly during winter each year. They enjoy an exposed position in the sun's hottest rays by day and at night the winter chill of their homelands.

With about 170 recorded species and varieties, and a size range from 12 in (30 cm) to 31 ft (9.5 m), puyas can make an interesting addition to any collection. Some of the puya species in cultivation are mentioned below.

Puya laxa is very spiny, heavily frosted in appearance, with irregular rosette growth. Except for its thorny habit, this small species with fuzzy foliage is almost tillandsia like, and makes an interesting container subject. It has a tall inflorescence with deep purple petals and is native to Bolivia, where it grows as a terrestrial in dry, stony soils.

Puya coerulea can reach 3¼ ft (1 m) in height at flowering. The flowers are dark blue. With silvery-white foliage this plant, although spiny, is most attractive. It is native to the central region of Chile, where it grows in dry, rocky terrain.

Puya pearcei is more serrated than spiny, with long, pliable, grey-green leaves. Its tall, branched inflorescence is much admired each winter and lasts over a very long period. The flowers are dark blue and green, turning to rose-red with age. The stems and bracts are frosted rose. This species, at least 3¼ ft (1 m) tall at flowering, grows slowly and is not invasive.

Puya venusta is another good plant for a collection. It requires a sunny position and well-drained compost. The semi-branched inflorescence has purple petals and a deep rose scape and bracts. This species is native to Chile.

Puya berteroniana and **Puya alpestris** are larger species with stunning flower colour combinations. Both are heavily spined, so position them in a sunny, roomy corner away from pedestrian traffic. At flowering time the beauty of these plants is unsurpassed.

Puya chilensis, because of its size and spreading habit, is more suitable for large displays and not advised for situations where space limitations are a problem.

Generally speaking, all puyas are practically indestructible and quite undemanding.

Quesnelia

Quesnelias are indigenous to the central coastal regions of Brazil. They can be found growing as epiphytes, low on trees or on rock outcrops, in the mountains bordering the coastline of this area. At a glance these species could be mistaken for those of *Billbergia*; and they require similar culture.

Closer to the coast in swampy lowlands, with some tree cover from the strongest sun rays, are the larger species with rosette shape and tanks to hold water.

Basking in the tropical sun in view of the ocean are species somewhere between the two. Growing in fine white sand over thin layers of leaf mould, these can be found scattered over the dunes areas, appearing to be almost indestructible.

Very few quesnelias are in cultivation. They are not difficult to grow. All have spined leaves, but some are barely spiny at all. Their inflorescences are rather fleeting, lasting about two weeks, which is about as long as the average billbergia. The forms and colours of the inflorescences can be stunning in their beauty and more than make their existence worthwhile.

In cultivation, quesnelias enjoy bright light to full sun but will tolerate areas of lower light. They require winter warmth and an open, well-drained compost and moderate water, with less during cold periods.

The mountain or higher altitude species are generally the easiest to grow. Of these *Quesnelia liboniana* should be more widely cultivated. As it offsets on stolons, it can be mounted, or grown in a basket. If placed at the base of a bromeliad tree *Quesnelia liboniana* attaches to the trunk and slowly climbs its new host. In habitat this species grows low in trees or on rock outcrops. Its flowers are navy blue and orange, an exotic combination.

Hardy and very adaptable to mounting is the lovely *Quesnelia marmorata*. With tube-like form heavily marbled maroon on grey-green, the slightly pendent inflorescence has rose-pink bracts and china blue petals.

In cultivation but not seen as frequently as the above, *Quesnelia lateralis* is named because of the habit of flowering from the base. Of easy culture in bright, filtered light, its leaves are green and the inflorescence has flame-red bracts and ming blue petals. It captivates all who see it.

The dwarf *Quesnelia humilis*, of tubular form with green foliage, is another of easy culture. With offsets on stolons this species adapts well to hanging pot or basket, or mounted on bark. It requires medium to bright, filtered light. The bracts are brilliant red, the petals are bright cerise.

Of the larger rosette types, *Quesnelia arvensis* and *Quesnelia quesneliana* are the most frequently seen in cultivation. Each grow well in bright, filtered light for more compact growth, but adapt well to medium light. In habitat *Quesnelia quesneliana* grows in full tropical sun close to the ocean's edge. *Quesnelia arvensis* is from the more moist, swampy areas. Both seem to produce at least two offsets before flowering, so it is wise not to divide them too frequently. Their large, cylinder-shaped inflorescence with no obvious stem is of deep rose to red in colour. The bracts arranged in shingle form appear like crimped crepe paper. The petals are mauve with white edge, or blue. Both plants have decorative white bands on the leaf reverse.

Quesnelia testudo grows in coastal scrub at sea level and offsets on obvious stolons. It has a less open rosette and a slimmer cylindric inflorescence on an obvious stem.

Streptocalyx

Of medium to large size, these plants are indigenous to areas of Guiana, Ecuador, Bolivia, Peru, Colombia and tropical Brazil. Not unlike the genus *Aechmea*, streptocalyx are of rosette form with spined leaves. The exotic inflorescence with often large, long-lasting bracts, usually a brilliant rose-red with blue or violet petals, often makes us attempt to grow these beautiful plants in our collections.

Streptocalyx are tropical plants and as such require winter warmth and humidity with medium to bright, filtered light. All streptocalyx are epiphytic and an open potting medium is essential, with just enough water in winter to prevent dehydration.

The giant *Streptocalyx floribundus* has been collected from areas of near sea level as far south as Espirito Santo extending to Rio de Janeiro and is suitable only for larger greenhouses or conservatories because of its immense size.

Occasionally cultivated are *Streptocalyx subnuda*, *Streptocalyx poeppigii* (Plate 42), *Streptocalyx longifolius* and *Streptocalyx holmesii* (Plate 43).

Only attempt to grow these beautiful plants if you are prepared to provide the extra winter care they must have to survive.

Wittrockia

This small genus is found only in the southern coastal regions of Brazil from near sea level extending to the coastal mountain ranges. Only two forms have found their way into cultivation.

First is the somewhat spiny *Wittrockia superba* with distribution from the states of Rio de Janeiro to Santa Catarina where it grows as an epiphyte, saxicolous and as a terrestrial, from almost sea level. This beautiful, stiff-leaved, well-armed plant needs bright conditions and makes a lovely pot specimen for large spaces. Its leaves are a glossy green with red tips and sharp terminal spines. The inflorescence, nestled in the heart of the plant, has startling red bracts and white petals and stays colourful for many months.

The soft-leaved and much smaller *Wittrockia smithii* comes from the southern Brazilian states of Parana and Santa Catarina. It resembles a nidularium and is of similar culture. It grows at medium altitudes in trees, on rocks, or in leaf litter on the ground. *Wittrockia smithii* has bi-coloured leaves with green above and tan-red reverse. The long-lasting floral bracts are brick red, the petals green and white.

Of easy culture, the wittrockias like an open, porous compost and partial shade.

CHAPTER 16

PROPAGATION

Propagation can be carried out in two ways; by vegetative offsets and by seeds. Compared to reproduction by seed, the vegetative process is by far the more rapid means of propagation. However, despite a longer time being require for plants to reach maturity from seed, the method has its reward with the production of much larger quantities.

Another method of propagation is meristem or tissue culture. Techniques are continuing to develop and as time progresses more and more plants will be propagated in this way.

Vegetative Propagation

Under good growing conditions a pup will flower two years after being separated from the parent. The latter flowers once, produces offsets and dies. This can take from one to two years, depending on the health of the parent and the number of pups produced. Some growers feed the parent plants in the hope of obtaining more offsets. Whether this is an advantage or not is open to question.

The offsets or pups are produced in the leaf axils at the base of the parent plant. They should be removed when one-third of the size of the parent, otherwise the latter will keep feeding them and not produce so many pups. It is preferable for the offset to have a firm, brown base before being removed. Its age can vary from three months onwards, depending on the health of the parent, its growth, habit, climatic conditions, etc. The first offsets produced are always the strongest. The more pups the parent produces, the weaker the offspring become.

Some pups can be removed from the parent by holding the latter firmly in one hand and gently moving the offspring from left to right with the other hand. This method operates best with plants which are inclined to be stoloniferous, that is, on stolons or runners. No force should be used, as the pup can easily snap off, leaving its lower part still attached to the mother. New growers, with no experience in removing offsets, should play safe and use secateurs to cut off the pup.

For those offsets which are closely attached to the mother, a saw-edged knife is the best instrument to use, cutting as closely as possible to the parent, without damaging the soft tissue of the latter. Damage to the caudex (trunk) of the parent plant will encourage bacterial or fungal attack, the same applying to the pup, if it is cut short. In all cases, the cut on the pup and the parent should be dusted with sulphur or some other fungicide. It takes many months for an offset to recover from too short a cut, as it has to grow a callous over the wound before it can send out roots. An analogy would be that of a premature baby.

In some species it is difficult to remove an offset. For example, *Vriesea splendens* offsets in the centre of the parent plant, beside the dying inflorescence. *Guzmania sanguinea* has the same characteristic. It takes courage to remove an offset such as this, as some part of the parent's 'soft' tissue must be taken with the pup. The former can die and also the offset. If only one pup is thrown, it is advisable to leave it on the parent. Gradually the pup will take over from the latter and when well established, the parent can be cut back and the root growth trimmed so that the offset can be planted deeper in the mixture. Better to save one plant than risk losing two plants. However, instances have occurred where growers have successfully removed the single pup and have been blessed with more progeny for their courage! When *Vriesea splendens* sends out two pups from its centre, cut the parent down the centre, giving half of the caudex and roots to each pup. Dust each half with fungicide before replanting. This method has been quite successful with no losses occurring.

After cutting, the base of the pup should be allowed to dry out for at least 24 hours before planting in damp peat moss or sand. There are many media used to induce roots on offsets. Some growers prefer vermiculite as this is a sterile product. It must be kept moist but not allowed to become waterlogged. Young, tender roots need some moisture to stay alive and grow. The plantings should be misted daily, except in very cold weather. It is better to be cold and dry, than cold and wet.

Those pups considered special, or needing a little extra care, can be placed in a polystyrene box, filled to a depth of 3–3½ in (7–8 cm) with damp peat moss or sand.

Another method which has proved successful is to place each pup on a base of wet sphagnum moss in a plastic pot. This way the plant is supported by the sides of the pot, does not wobble about and feels secure. The pup's base is not buried in the moss but only rests on it. It does not take long for the offset to root in the darkness the pot affords. Excellent results have been obtained from this method, with rarely a plant being lost from basal rot.

Some bromeliads do not root easily after being separated from the parent. One species, notorious for its reluctance to produce roots, is

1 Wait until pup is about one-third size of parent

2 Sever with serrated blade knife or small pruning saw. Allow to dry for 1–2 days, then dust cut surfaces with fungicide before replanting

GROWING MEDIUM

3 Pot in preferred growing medium (see text)

4 Place plant in a light, airy position

Figure 14   Propagation by pup or offset

Neoregelia pendula. It is stoloniferous and can be rooted by planting in another pot with its parent before it has been severed from the latter. A slight nick on the underside of the stolon, dusted with fungicide, then pinned down on damp peat moss, will usually bring about the desired effect. When rooted, cut through the initial nick, dust again with fungicide. This method can also be applied to the stoloniferous aechmeas, such as *Aechmea chantinii* and its numerous forms.

It is considered bad husbandry to put offsets into the growing medium before they have grown roots. With no roots to anchor them they can topple over. The compost can harbour bacteria or fungi which attack the young plants before they can grow roots. They can also miss out when the plants around them are being watered, not possessing sufficient leaves to catch the water and convey it to their leaf axils.

Vegetative offsetting does not apply to all bromeliads. For example, some species of tillandsias do not pup at all, but produce copious seed to carry on the species.

Some other genera produce pups while still immature and long before they flower. *Vriesea glutinosa* is heir to this condition. An extension to this is *Aechmea gigantea*, which will offset readily, but will not flower at all, at least not in the writer's experience.

Seed Propagation

A quick way to enlarge your collection of bromeliads is to grow them from seed. It is a most interesting pursuit and occasionally the grower is blessed with a variegated seedling or an outstanding addition to the family. Seed from species breed true replicas of their parents, provided the seed has not been pollinated from another species or hybrid. Seed from hybrids or hybrids crossed with species is varied and unpredictable.

There are two different kinds of fruit and seeds in bromeliads. The seeds of one are contained in a berry-like fruit, and seeds of the other are in a hard capsule or pod that springs open when it is ripe.

Members of the subfamily Bromelioideae, which contains aechmeas, billbergias, neoregelias, nidulariums and cryptanthus, have their seed encased in berries. These contain a sticky, sweet jelly, particularly in the billbergias and cryptanthus, which have the largest seed of all. By comparison, aechmeas and neoregelias have very small seed. When the berries are ripe, ants and birds are attracted and will carry the seed away; nature's way of dispersal and starting new colonies of bromeliads. The seed is enriched by concentrations of nutrients, which will succour the seedlings until they can grow roots and obtain their own nutrition.

The fruits of most of the species which are berry-like will ripen in about three months. Many of them become softer and darker when they reach maturity and should be removed as soon as they are ripe. Billbergias have the shortest term — three months. Aechmeas are similar but there are exceptions: for example, *Aechmea fasciata* takes up to nine months. Nidulariums need four months to ripen their berries, neoregelias six months. Cryptanthus fruits should be watched. They ripen down in the leaf axils and if the fruits are not removed, the seeds will germinate there.

When seeds are gathered they should be carefully cleaned, dried and then placed in envelopes or small non-airtight containers which are labelled for identification and date of harvesting. Seeds of bromeliads may retain their viability for several months but rarely more than six months. For the best results they should be planted as soon as possible, preferably no later than three months.

Cleaning the seeds is quite important, as all the surrounding pulp must be removed to prevent decay. Otherwise the latter will rapidly destroy the tiny embryo in the seed. The berries can be mashed or their contents squeezed out on to absorbent paper towelling and the results spread out thinly on the paper. Carefully scrape the seeds off onto a new sheet of paper allowing as much of the pulp to remain on the old paper as possible. Repeat the process and then place the seeds on fresh paper to dry up the last traces of the pulp.

An alternative method is to squeeze the contents of the berries into a small jar of water fitted with a watertight lid. The jar containing water and seeds is then shaken and the resulting pulp/water mixture poured off, leaving the good seeds in the bottom of the jar. This procedure is repeated with more clean water. Finally pour off carefully and transfer the remaining small quantity containing the seeds on to a paper towel for drying.

In order to prevent the growth of fungus, dust the seed with fungicide or soak for a few moments in a fungicide solution followed by final drying on fresh paper towelling.

The Pitcairnioideae subfamily (pitcairnias, hechtias, dyckias, etc.) produces seeds in dry capsules or pods ½–1½ in (1–3 cm) long. The seeds are small and dry and do not require cleaning when removed from the pods.

Home-grown seed is always the best as it is fresh. Seed from overseas is suspect as the grower does not know how old it is and precious time can be wasted trying to germinate seed which has lost its viability in storage. However, instances have occurred where some seed will stay dormant for

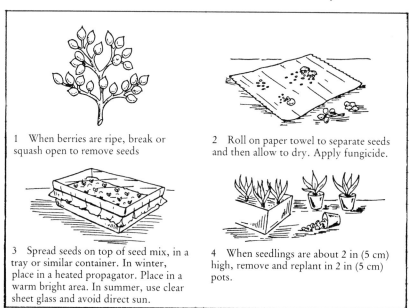

1 When berries are ripe, break or squash open to remove seeds

2 Roll on paper towel to separate seeds and then allow to dry. Apply fungicide.

3 Spread seeds on top of seed mix, in a tray or similar container. In winter, place in a heated propagator. Place in a warm bright area. In summer, use clear sheet glass and avoid direct sun.

4 When seedlings are about 2 in (5 cm) high, remove and replant in 2 in (5 cm) pots.

Figure 15 Propagation by seed

some months then burst into life when the grower has lost patience and is ready to throw it out. This particularly applies to cryptanthus seed. Seeds readily germinate with humidity and warmth. Temperatures from 68–86°F (20–30°C) are ideal.

Unless you are in the commercial field, it is well that you do not plant more than 30 seeds of each successful pollination. Too many seedlings is more of a chore than a labour of love. Surplus seeds should be distributed to friends to experiment with. Much pleasure can be derived in comparing notes on progress.

Each experienced grower has his or her own private mix when it comes to growing seeds. All parts of the mix must be put through a fine sieve. The seeds are so small, they could be lost in a rough mixture. A suggested combination is equal parts of charcoal, peat moss and sand. The charcoal is pounded and sieved, the fine parts are placed in the mix, while the rough pieces are placed in the bottom of the seed box to give good drainage. Charcoal has a purifying effect and will keep the mixture free from algae.

Wet the mixture with fungicide made up to half strength. Place the mixture on top of the coarse charcoal previously placed in the seed box, and gently tamp down. Spread the seed on top and wet with a fine spray using the half-strength fungicide. Label the seed with the name of the parent and the date of planting. If sowing in winter, place the container in a heated propagator to maintain minimum temperatures. If the seed is planted in summer a sheet of clear glass placed over the container is ideal. A thin layer of fine grit placed on the compost surface will prevent moss and algae from forming. Spray over with water when the seed mix looks dry, until the seedlings have established.

In 14 days or so, depending on the age of the seed and the warmth of the weather, you should be rewarded with the first signs of the seed germinating. When the seedlings have one or two leaves each, they should gradually be accustomed to general temperatures by slowly increasing the amount of ventilation. Do this until they are old enough to adapt to cooler air. The seedlings should be shaded from direct sunlight.

After a couple of months the faster growing seedlings such as billbergias should be planted in seed trays, 1 in (2.5 cm) or so apart, depending on their size. They can now benefit from a weak (half-strength or less) solution of foliar feed. Until the seedlings develop tanks to hold water and nutrition, they depend on their roots for most of their nutriment. Thus a good medium is essential for their growth and development. Equal quantities of fine pine bark, sand, charcoal and peat-based potting compost is ideal.

At six months the seedlings should be big enough for their own individual pots. Pebbles placed around their bases keep them stable and stop them wobbling about; the pebbles also keep the mixture moist around the young plants. It is preferable to use plastic pots, 2 in (5 cm) square or round, for the first planting. Clay pots dry out too quickly, and young roots quickly desiccate and die if not regularly watered. Bromeliad seedlings grow slower than most other plants and need to be potted on about once a year.

Do not foliar feed seedlings in the winter. Sudden temperature drops can kill soft, lush growth. Harder grown plants respond to foliar feeding in spring.

Not all bromeliads produce similar type of seed or require the same germination procedure. The subfamily Tillandsioideae contains, among others, the genera *Vriesea*, *Tillandsia* and *Guzmania*. All produce hard seed capsules or pods which are very slow ripening, and may take six to twelve months before maturity. At this stage the pods will burst open, discharging the tiny seeds into the atmosphere.

Since the seeds are dry with no pulp surrounding them when the pods have burst open, they do not need cleaning as described earlier. Measuring from 1/32–¼ in (1–7 mm) long, they are very fine, with a slender tail attached from which spider-like hairs branch out to form a type of parachute. In their native habitat they are carried great distances by the wind until they fasten to a suitable host.

To harvest the seed one needs to be observant and collect it before it disperses into the air, particularly with plants grown near vents. Comments have been made earlier concerning storage. It is emphasised that fresh, viable seed is essential for good germination and this may take from two to six months in some species.

Guzmanias, vrieseas and some green-leaf forms of tillandsias (*Tillandsia complanata* and *Tillandsia viridiflora*) can be sown in a similar manner to aechmeas and billbergias, using a similar compost and conditions for germination.

Most tillandsia seeds require an entirely different approach. There are a number of ways in which seed may be sown. It may be spread over a slab of cork bark or on the top of sphagnum moss placed in a container. Another method is to secure the seeds around a length of florists' driftwood by winding light nylon fishing line from end to end of the branch. This will hold the seeds in place until they firmly attach themselves. Some growers use a polystyrene box with a piece of muslin arched inside, or stretched across the top, over which the seeds are spread. Their little 'parachutes' of hairs stick to the open weave of the cloth. Experiment to see which method gives the best results.

Sow the seeds in a sheltered area free of draughts, otherwise the seed can be caught in gusts of air and be lost. Mist over the seeds with water and place or hang in a shaded position with ample air circulation. If possible, sow seeds in spring or summer for best germination. Some species will produce seed in autumn or winter, and these should be germinated in a heated propagator. Mist them twice daily in very hot weather and in winter once every second day will be sufficient, depending on temperature. Tillandsias need good air circulation and should be allowed to dry out between mistings.

Observe the progress of the tiny plants, which are just green specks when they first emerge, and use your own judgement as to watering. The seedlings are very slow growing, so be patient, it may take two or three years before they are large enough to remove for remounting.

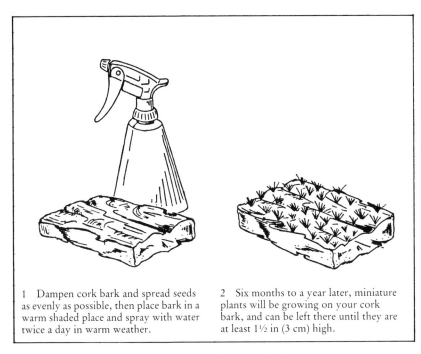

1 Dampen cork bark and spread seeds as evenly as possible, then place bark in a warm shaded place and spray with water twice a day in warm weather.

2 Six months to a year later, miniature plants will be growing on your cork bark, and can be left there until they are at least 1½ in (3 cm) high.

Figure 16   Propagation of *Tillandsia* seed on cork bark

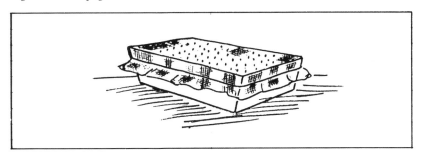

Figure 17   Propagation of *Tillandsia* on muslin. Seeds are spread on muslin stretched over a container.

Hybridising

The inflorescences of bromeliads are many and varied. In some genera they can last a year, retaining their colour and shape. Others are short-lived, such as billbergias, whose spikes last for only a week or so.

The individual flowers survive for only two or three days. Usually it is the bracts which contain the colour and these can last for many months, particularly in the aechmeas, neoregelias and nidulariums.

The inflorescence varies from being simple to complex. Some have hundreds of flowers, while others bear only a few. Aechmeas and billbergias have brightly coloured bracts which grow along the flower stalks to protect the flower branches as they emerge from the sheaths. Neoregelias flower low down in the water of their cups and to pollinate these it is necessary to remove the water to get to the seed-bearing parts.

Before one embarks on a programme of hybridisation it is necessary to learn the names of, and to recognise, the parts of the flower. The whole base on which the flower rests and to which it is attached, is called the calyx. All bromeliad flowers have three petals, enclosed or contained by three sepals. Flower petals come in many colours. These petals surround the sexual part of the flower. Inside the petals are six stamens, topped by boat-like structures called anthers, which are the male parts. In the centre of all is the pistil, which is topped by the female part called the stigma. This can be much longer than the stamens, as in billbergias, or it can be enclosed like a dome by stamens, making it difficult to hybridise successfully.

It is 'love's labour lost' to try to cross self-pollinating flowers. This means that the female part of the flower, called the stigma, is receptive only to its own pollen.

In the billbergias, self-pollination is difficult as the stigma is extended

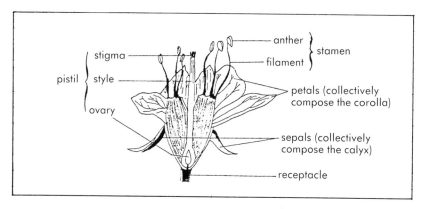

Figure 18   Structure of a typical bromeliad flower

well out from the pollen anthers and it takes an insect such as a bee or an ant, or the wind, to convey the pollen to it. But with human intervention the process of self- or cross-pollination is easy.

Cryptanthus is easy to hybridise by cross-pollination. Cryptanthus have male flowers which appear first in the centres of the plants and later the female flowers appear in the upper leaf axils. These female flowers also have anthers, bearing pollen, but it is probable that this pollen is infertile, otherwise members of this genus would set more seed than they naturally do. This leads to the conclusion that nature's intention is not for self-pollination, as the male flowers have withered and died before the female flowers appear.

Neoregelias and aechmeas are the most difficult to hybridise because the flowers are so small, with the anthers closing over the stigma as if protecting it from any intruder. The anthers must be removed, preferably before the pollen is mature. Once ripe, the pollen can fall off or blow on to the stigma and you can be left with a self-pollinated flower and miss out on the cross-fertilised seed you had intended.

Having established that the plant whose flowers you wish to cross-pollinate is not self-pollinating, gather the pollen from another plant. This will be the male side of the cross. After removing the pollen, store it in the refrigerator, where it should keep viable for some months. Fresh pollen is best to use, but refrigeration is necessary as plants do not all flower at the same time. Always label your pollen with the name of the plant from which you took it, and the date so that you can discard it when the pollen is some months old and probably not viable any longer.

Gently remove the anthers of the female side of the cross. The petals of the flower can be pushed aside, but must not be removed, since they close over the stigma as the flower withers. Anthers can easily be cut away with scissors on billbergias or cryptanthus, but neoregelias and aechmeas need forceps to perform the operation. It can be done with scissors, but it is a clumsier method as the pollen can be easily spilled on to the stigma. If this happens, instead of your chosen cross you end up with replicas of the mother plant or, if one or more parents are hybrids, you can obtain varied seedlings.

The period during which the flower is fully open is called anthesis, mostly occurring around 10 a.m. Some genera have anthesis at night, when they are pollinated by moths. The stigma, or female part, is receptive to pollen for only a short while and this is indicated by small globules of glistening, sticky 'honey dew' on the stigma.

Use a glass rod or another similar implement to deposit the pollen on the stigma. If the pollen won't stick, wet the end with your tongue and the pollen will adhere. Some growers use an artist's brush to transfer pollen, but this is not recommended because of the possibility of inadvertent pollen transfer from some previous pollinating programme.

Label the flower of the female plant with the name of the pollen plant, and the date of the cross, making sure the label is secure, as hosing or watering can send your tag awash and cause it to disappear. It is impossible to rely on your memory. It is important that these details, together with the date of first flowering of the progeny are recorded for future reference. If you achieve something spectacular in your seedlings, this information is vital for other hybridists and botanists to work from.

After some months you will know if your efforts have been successful. In neoregelias, the green sepals which encase the seed capsule are visible in the water. Flowers which have not impregnated turn brown and mushy. In aechmeas, successful pollination is demonstrated by the berries turning a vivid colour, usually blue. When the capsule is ripe, it will come away easily from its attachment to the calyx. Do not try to force it, as this will mean the seed is still immature.

Choose your parents wisely. Do not hybridise haphazardly just because two plants are blooming at the same time. Choose parents that you think can be improved by better colour, better form or more leaves. Plants which are susceptible to cold burn can be improved by hybridising with others which are low temperature tolerant. Perhaps a miniature would make a better hanging basket specimen if it had stolons, and so on.

CHAPTER 17

BIOLOGY OF
BROMELIADS

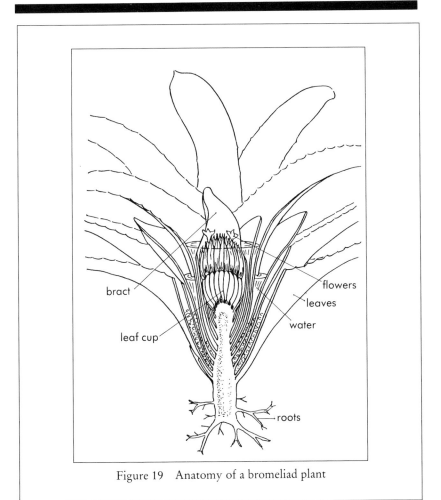

Figure 19   Anatomy of a bromeliad plant

It is the purpose of this chapter to discuss some of the adaptive strategies that have allowed bromeliads to colonise often hostile environments successfully, and also to acquaint the reader with some aspects of basic bromeliad biology.

Bromeliads can be described in general terms as a group of stress-tolerant herbaceous perennials with a pronounced tendency towards epiphytism and saxicoly. Whether growing on trees hosts, on rocks or in soil, a large majority of bromeliad species populates habitats characterised by at least one, but more commonly by a combination of physical restraints; sunlight is frequently excessive, whereas water and nutrients are usually in short supply for at least part of the year.

A characteristic, universal to all bromeliads equipping them to deal effectively with one or more of the mentioned physical restraints, is the presence of trichomes (coloquially termed 'scales' by bromeliad growers) on many leaf surfaces. Trichomes (Figure 20) are epidermal appendages, usually hair-like, common to many plants, but it is the modified, peculiar kind of shield-like trichome observed on all bromeliads that was taken as evidence that, despite their many differences, pitcairnioids, bromelioids and tillandsioids are closely enough related to be placed into a single family.

However, the function of the trichome on the leaf shoots has become more modified as one compares more primitive members of the family with more specialised ones. In many pitcairnioids, for example, which take up water and nutrients from the soil via their root system, trichomes are simple in structure and mainly located on the undersides of leaves around the stomata or leaf pores as a protective device against transpiration or water loss. In most bromelioids, but also in many water and nutrient impounding tank-type tillandsioids, trichomes have become more complex in their structural arrangement and have reached their greatest accumulation in the region of the tank where they now function in an analogue manner to roots in more conventional plants by absorbing water and nutrients. But trichomes have achieved the highest degree of structural complexity with elaborately winged shield cells in the atmospheric tillandsias (plants that live exclusively from the humidity and nutrients present in the air) and in some vrieseas (e.g. *Vriesea espinosae*), which are often so densely covered by them that the plants appear grey or silvery-white when dry. To allow these plants to survive and flourish in what could be considered a no-man's land for life, the basic concept of trichomes has been exploited in several important ways to aid survival — to reflect high intensity light effectively which would otherwise burn the sensitive tissue and organs of the plant, to shield the leaf pores against water loss and effectively to intercept and absorb moisture and dissolved nutrients from the surrounding atmosphere.

By making the adaptive shift towards epiphytism or saxicoly, many

Figure 20   Bromeliad trichomes seen from above (highly magnified)

bromeliads have minimised the pressures of competition for space, light and nutrients experienced by soil-growing plants and have crossed the frontier beyond which plant life of conventional design and performance could not exist. In the branches of a host tree or on the surface of rocks, roots no longer fulfil the purpose of procuring water and nutrients from the substrate and so are modified into organs of anchorage, which under the circumstances have a much greater survival value. In some tillandsia species, for example, where the plants can secure themselves firmly in the branches of their hosts by virtue of tendril-like leaves (e.g. *Tillandsia duratii, T. usneoides*), roots are generally only produced in seedlings and later abandoned altogether for the possible reason of strict economy.

For bromeliads, which entrap water and nutrients in a central tank formed by the leaves arranged in a tight rosette, upright growth is a functional necessity, but not all bromeliads are restricted to this growth habit. In extreme atmospheric tillandsias for example, the need to respond to gravitational pull, which in conventional plants guides the roots to enter the soil (positive geotropism) to procure minerals and water for the wellbeing of the plant and compels the shoots and leaves to grow away from the soil (negative geotropism) towards the light to enable photosynthesis, is no longer a necessity for survival. The response to geotropism has been largely abandoned, allowing such species to colonise even the underside of branches, a venue which further reduces competition for space from other more conventional epiphytes and provides shade and shelter from sun and weather.

Most epiphytes, but particularly atmospheric tillandsias and some of the vrieseas which qualify for similar status, face dramatic nutritional problems. Most nutrients are located in the soil, but these plants grow attached to trees and rocks which as substrates are quite infertile. The only nutrients available to these plants are those dissolved in precipitation such as rainwater and intercepted by the plant's trichomes. These plants usually possess compact bodies with low surface-to-volume ratios which further complicates the matter of nutrient procurement in sufficient quantity. While a low surface-to-volume ratio effectively reduces water loss during periods of drought, it is poorly designed to enhance nutrient gain. Minerals must be absorbed through a very small surface considering the volume of tissues requiring supply. Furthermore, since atmospherics dry rapidly they must absorb nutrients quickly while still wet. In essence, atmospherics had to evolve strategies of strict nutrient economy not only to survive, but to flourish on nutrient levels which would be well below the minimum requirements of more conventional plants.

Carbohydrates such as sugars, starches and cellulose not only play an essential part in the life functions of all organisms in one way or another, but cellulose in particular is the principal structural component in plants, and starch the principal stored food. Carbohydrates are, for the sake of simplicity, complex molecules of C (Carbon), O (Oxygen) and H (Hydrogen) which are synthesised by plants with the aid of absorbed sun or light energy from such simple molecules as CO (carbon dioxide) and H_O (water) in the process known as photosynthesis.

Conventional plants photosynthesise during the daytime when the necessary light energy is available and at the same time supply the building blocks of carbohydrates to the synthesis process — water from the soil via the root system or from water storage tissue within the plant, and carbon dioxide taken up by diffusion via the widely opened stomata. During this process water will be unavoidably diffused out of the leaf from the stomata, which are actively involved in carbon dioxide up-take, and therefore lost to the plant. Such water loss, which seems expendable in conventional plants growing in habitats where moisture is more readily available, would lead to fatal desiccation in most plants growing under arid conditions where water is not a readily renewable resource.

Most drought-enduring bromeliads and orchids, but also cacti and many other desert plants, have broken with the conventional principles of photosynthesis. They only open their stomata at night to take up carbon dioxide from the atmosphere, at a time of relative coolness during which water loss by evaporation from the leaf pores is minimal. The carbon dioxide thus captured in the absence of light is stored by converting it into simple organic non-gaseous compounds, most notably malic acid which is also a common fruit constituent.

Much less energy is needed to convert carbon dioxide into malic acid than into equivalent amounts of carbohydrate and the energy required temporarily to fix carbon dioxide is obtained by the plant breaking down some of its starch reserves. At daybreak the leaf pores close and the stored pool of malic acid is gradually degraded by enzymes, liberating carbon dioxide into the leaf interior where it remains trapped by the now nearly impervious foliar surface. As the sun's energy is absorbed by the plant's leaf surface, photosynthesis occurs, fed by the regenerated carbon dioxide and vital carbohydrates are synthesised.

This process of carbon fixation is known as Crassulacean Acid Metabolism (CAM) as it was first discovered in succulents of the family Crassulaceae. Although this kind of carbon dioxide fixation and subsequent photosynthesis is not as efficient in terms of carbohydrate production when compared to the more familiar photosynthetic pathway employed by more conventional plants, it is a very effective survival strategy to prevent water loss in an arid environment.

It is the sum total of adaptive mechanisms that has turned many bromeliads into superb survival 'machines' and has differentiated them from other plants. They appeal to the eye through their diversity of body form, leaf coloration and flowers — and to the mind by being unique in many fascinating ways.

Physiological adaptations may have allowed bromeliads to survive as individuals in hostile environments and to minimise competition from other plants for available resources, but it is the biological phenomenon of reproduction common to all life, the successful passing on of acquired traits to the progeny that ultimately determines the survival of the species. In this context, success is measured by the number of viable offspring produced, and by the degree of survival guarantees each offspring is provided with to reach sexual maturity itself.

In general, each bromeliad plant is equipped to produce a reasonable number of seeds as potential starting points for a new generation. But as bromeliad seed viability is relatively short, and as dispersed seeds depend very much on the chance encounter with a suitable substrate and the right growth-supporting climate for successful germination and maturation, the provided survival guarantees for bromeliad offspring seem somewhat limited.

Most bromeliads produce by both sexual and asexual means. Seeds result from the sexual process and offshoots from asexual reproduction. Only the sexual reproduction process allows genetic material from different parents to be combined in the offspring. Asexually produced offshoots are genetically identical to their parent. Since each bromeliad plant usually flowers and sets seeds only once, the ability to produce offshoots by asexual reproduction must be considered beneficial for species survival. This is because the process of flowering and seed production can be repeated as each offshoot matures, thus increasing the chance for seeds from a given plant eventually to find suitable conditions for germination and continued growth.

Gene recombination through the sexual process is necessary to assure that a species maintains some genetic heterogeneity and therefore a certain degree of evolutionary flexibility. Without this it would have little chance of adjusting to the changes that take place in all habitats.

Flowers are the sexual organs of the higher plants. They are, in effect, modified shoots charged with the production of sex cells called eggs and sperm. Most bromeliad flowers bear both sexual and sterile appendages, and as flowers cannot move about to seek and sexually fertilise each other, they produce visual signals, scents and rewards to attract animal go-betweens which act as pollinators.

The bromeliad flower is in its organisation typical of most flowers (Figure 6). It is composed of the tip of a stem called the receptacle and four types of floral organs which grow from it. These are usually borne in whorls separated by very short internodes.

The floral arrangement contains two groups of sterile structures; the sepals, collectively called the calyx, are the lowermost set of floral organs which usually enclose and protect the other flower parts in the bud. Sepals are usually green, small and leaf-like in shape. The petals, collectively called the corolla and which constitute the next whorl of structures, are often the most conspicuous part of the flower. By virtue of their bright colours, sweetish nectar and distinctive floral odours they provide many powerful signals to potential animal pollinators.

Within the circumference of the corolla are the stamens, each usually consisting of a slender stalk or filament bearing at its tip an enlarged portion, the anther, which produces pollen. Surrounded by the stamens at the centre of the flower is the pistil composed of an enlarged lower portion, the ovary (which contains one or more eggs or ovules each with the potential to become a seed); the style, a slender structure rising from the ovary; and the expanded tip of the style called the stigma. It is within the anther and within the ovary that sex cells or gametes are produced in a process not unlike that in the ovaries and testes of animals.

The Austrian Augustinian-abbot and scientist, Gregor Mendel (1822–1884), was the first person to demonstrate conclusively that inherited characteristics are controlled by discrete units called genes, which are passed from one generation to the next in the sexual process.

To understand the significance of the sexual process in relation to heredity, one has to understand certain aspects of cellular phenomena called mitosis and meiosis.

The bodies of plants and animals are made up of cells which may number many millions in higher life forms. All cells which make up the body of the organism have a cell nucleus which contains the genetic material, the chromosomes, which determines the shape, colour, size, resistance to disease, and all the other characteristics of the individual. The chromosomes in the nuclei of normal body cells occur in corresponding pairs in which each member of a pair resembles its corresponding partner or homologue without being necessarily totally identical. Body cells with chromosome pairs are called diploid cells.

The characteristic number of chromosomes in body cells of plants and animals varies widely from species to species. For instance, the genus *Cryptanthus* has 34, several pitcairnias have 50 and a number of neoregelias possess 54. Growth and body repair involves division of an existing body cell into two daughter cells which each in turn will divide again into two daughter cells, and so forth. In the event of this type of cell division the double set of genetic material is replicated by the cell and passed on to the daughter cells. This process is termed mitosis. All of the body cells of an organism are therefore genetically identical.

In the production of sex cells—eggs and sperm—the same principle applies, but with the difference that only one half of a corresponding chromosome pair is passed on to the resulting daughter cells. This type of cell division is termed meiosis, and sex cells, for reason of having only a half set of chromosomes, are called haploid.

In higher plants such as bromeliads, the event of pollination has to occur prior to fertilisation. Liberation of pollen grains and their transmittal by suitable vectors—in bromeliads these are usually insects, birds and bats—to the stigma of flowers of the same plant (self-pollination) or other plants of the same species (cross-pollination) marks the beginning of the process of sexual reproduction.

After being deposited on the stigma, the pollen grain absorbs food and water and sends forth a pollen tube which grows downwards through the style and into the ovary, where it finally penetrates the embryo sac surrounding the egg cell to discharge its male or sperm nuclei. Fertilisation—fusion of haploid sperm and egg cell—can now occur. The resulting diploid zygote, by the process of cell division and differentiation, shortly develops into an embryo.

During its development, the embryo with its endosperm or storage tissue and integument or outer covering, receives food material from the parent plant. These foods—for the most part starches, oils and proteins—which accumulate in the endosperm will be utilised by the embryo when the seed subsequently germinates into a young plant. At the same time, while the seeds are forming, the ovary also increases in size and the outer flower parts—stamens, petals and sepals—deteriorate and are discarded. Thus, the enlarging ovary with its developing seeds becomes the fruit.

Bromeliads, like almost all higher plants, are sessile, and to transfer pollen from one flower to another requires an external mobile agent.

Many plants, like cycads, most grasses and conifers, use the wind to carry pollen to the receptive stigmas of other flowers. The prerequisites for successful wind pollination are large quantities of light, powdery pollen produced by the anthers and expansive, feathery stigmas to strain any passing pollen grains out of the air currents. No wind pollination has so far been recognised amongst bromeliads, but some *Hechtia* species are being considered as possibilities.

The vast majority of bromeliads employs animals as pollinators. To do this successfully, the flowers of these plants have to produce visual signals, scents and rewards to which these animals are responsive.

Birds, particularly humming birds, are the most common visitors to bromeliad flowers. Typical bird-pollinated bromeliads possess odourless flowers equipped with long, sturdy, tubular corollas. Both anthers and stigma usually protrude from the corolla to ensure that sticky pollen will adhere to the pollinator's forehead, whence it can be transferred to another stigma. Bird-pollinated flowers produce large quantities of nectar, and signal their presence with contrast colours such as red, yellow and violet, but particularly through vivid shades of red in both petals and bracts, a colour to which the bird's eye is exceptionally sensitive.

Similarly shaped flowers of pastel to dark green shades, which are most fragrant after sunset, are usually pollinated by moths.

Perfumed white, yellow or lavender flowers in which the corolla tube is short, and where anthers and stigma rarely extend beyond the throat of the corolla, are usually pollinated by butterflies, bees and allied insects.

Bat pollinated bromeliad species are confined to the tropics. Flowers designed to attract blossom bats are usually large, or several smallish blossoms are clustered into dense inflorescences. Corolla colours are varied, ranging from white to brown. These flowers signal to flower bats with scents reminiscent of fermenting fruit, and reward the pollinators with abundant nectar and pollen. As with all animal pollinators, the pollen is lodged on the bat's body and transferred to the stigma when the animal visits another flower.

Most plants, including bromeliads, preclude self-pollinating and favour biparental reproduction, and pollen from the same plant or from its asexually produced offsets may not produce fertilisation. Yet many bromeliads are self-compatible and, although self-pollination is often delayed by either initial spatial separation of anthers and stigma on a flower or by time delays between maturation of stamens or pistils, self-pollination may ultimately occur as a fail-safe device if animal cross-pollination is denied. This occurs by anthers and stigma coming close together or by remaining viable or receptive for long enough for self-pollination and fertilisation to eventuate.

To take self-pollination to the extreme, some bromeliads, in an apparent defiance of the rule that all organisms must outcross at least now and then, manage without pollinator service of any kind. Flowers of such plants never open (cleistogamy) and their pollen is simply shed on to a closely adjacent stigma within an unopened corolla.

After successful pollination, a distinct structure called fruit, containing the seed or seeds, is formed. The purpose of the fruit is to protect the seeds, and frequently to aid in their dispersal. Depending on species and prevailing climatic conditions, the fruit of bromeliads require between three months and over one year to reach maturity. Bromeliads produce essentially two kinds of fruit: Tillandsioideae and Pitcairnioideae form elongated, often several-centimetre-long capsules which become dry at maturity and split open to release the seed; Bromelioideae generally produce fleshy berries, often vividly coloured and of high sugar content, which rely to a large extent on fruit-eating animals for seed dispersal. The most complex of the Bromelioideae fruit type is the one produced by *Ananas* and *Pseudananas* where each diamond-shaped section of the pineapple represents the product of a single flower which, during development fuses with adjacent sections to form a multiple fruit.

Seed shape, size and number per fruit vary significantly in Bromeliaceae. Seeds of pitcairnioids are mostly very small, triangular to fusiform, often equipped with wing-like appendages; they are primarily dispersed by wind and flowing water. Tillandsioid seeds are $\frac{1}{32}$–$\frac{1}{4}$ in (1–7 mm) long, spindle-shaped, and each seed is equipped with extensive unbranched coma hairs which allow the seed to be carried by wind to rough surfaces like rocks and tree bark. The seed of Bromelioideae are generally small, elongated, ovoid or pear-shaped structures; as bromelioid berries are an important food source for many animals, particularly fruit-eating birds, the contained hard seed will generally pass unharmed through the animal's digestive system to be eventually eliminated with the excreta.

Bromeliad seed in general lose their viability relatively quickly. For the majority of bromeliads maximum germination is only realised if the seeds are not older than three months since maturation, but some seeds may retain viability for up to six months. Studies have shown that seeds of some xerophytic bromeliads (growing in arid regions) have remained viable for over one year. This fact has distinct survival values when one considers that seeds of such plants must be able to survive over long climatically adverse intervals to take advantage of those infrequent occasions when conditions are conducive to germination.

Factors which have a significant bearing on the longevity of bromeliad seeds are the rate of metabolic activity during the quiescent stage, and the degree of associated biochemical activity. The bromeliad enthusiast who wishes to grow plants from seed must be aware that a warm storage temperature will generally accelerate metabolic and chemical reactions within the seed, leading to a premature loss of viability. Total exclusion of oxygen would also lead to the seed's premature death, and seed storage in sealed containers or wrapping in plastic is not recommended.

To maximise longevity, bromeliad seeds are therefore best maintained in a cool and relatively dry environment where they preferably should be stored wrapped in tissue paper.

CHAPTER 18

VARIEGATION IN BROMELIADS

Throughout the plant kingdom variegation is widespread, appearing in many families including strong representation in the Bromeliaceae. In the broadest sense variegation means simply a diversity of two or more colours. This definition could apply to 60 to 70 per cent of all cultivated bromeliads with their crossbands, spots, stripes, blotches, fenestrations, bronze and pink leaf markings upon foliage of one plain tone (not necessarily green). However, the term as applied here and accepted in horticulture is confined to varieties and cultivars displaying leaf blades with longitudinal stripes of contrasting colours.

Possibly over 100 different variegates have appeared amongst bromeliads to date, with more emerging periodically in collections around the world. Considering the number and variety of bromeliads growing in the wild, variegation occurs very rarely. In most isolated cases the offspring, if highly variegated, survive only through man's intervention by collecting. One notable exception are the colonies of *Guzmania monostachia* var. *variegata* located in the Fahkahatchee Swamp of the Florida Everglades. Variegates occur very rarely in the subfamily Pitcairnioideae and infrequently in the Tillandsioideae, restricted to the genera *Guzmania*, *Vriesea* and, to a lesser extent, *Tillandsia*. Variegation is predominant in the Bromelioideae, especially *Aechmea*, *Ananas*, *Billbergia*, *Cryptanthus*, *Neoregelia* and *Nidularium*. At least several dozen *Aechmea* variegates are recorded, but the specific reasons for this large concentration in a genus have not been determined.

Causes of Variegation

The controversy has been debated for years and despite advances in modern scientific research comparatively little is known of the causes specifically in bromeliads. Botanists generally agree that bromeliads are rather unstable in their genetic construction and for this reason the following theories, outlined briefly, are considered plausible.

Viruses abound in the plant and animal world and have long been held responsible for many crippling and destructive diseases. Their role in nature is largely seen as the quality controllers of living organisms. These micropathogens or viroids have the ability to alter the genetic programming of plant cells by molecular insertion and extraction of chromosomal pieces. Bromeliads are known to harbour viral pathogens but the relationship and mechanics of viruses to the plant's physiology is poorly understood. It is thought viruses attack the apical and intercalary meristems or the central vascular core. As monocotyledons, bromeliads have mostly parallel-veined leaves and as new growth is initiated in these regions, the affected cells reproduce the striped sections we see. Micropathogens are known to gain entry through lesions in leaves, roots or rhizomes brought on by mechanical injury. Not all viruses are transmitted by vectors (carriers) such as animals, insects (400 species), mites, aphids, nematodes and other soil-inhabiting organisms such as fungi. For variegation to arise by seed, it is believed the mature plant in flower must be infected before the ovules are fertilised or possibly by the pollen being virus-infected if cross-pollination occurs. Viruses are often no longer present in a host once the symptoms are evident.

Environmental factors are frequently cited as probable causes of variegation but conclusive proof has not been established. Some scientists propose that one biological effect of natural radiation is gene mutation, as plant foliage and roots absorb radioactive substances. In laboratory experiments with gamma and x-rays, after irradiation there occurs a reduction in the number of cells per meristem. This reduction varies directly with the proportion of cells showing chromosome damage. DNA content and chromosomal size are considered important contributing factors. Chemical mutagens are capable of producing plant variegation; flower-inducing compounds such as BOH and Omaflora have promoted variegated offsets from mature rosettes.

Correlated factors in micro-climates (temperature, moisture and light) are often advanced as influential forces in creating variegation. Where occurring in a native habitat, some theorists hold that this exemplifies evolution in progress. Abiotic stress, where a plant suffers prolonged dehydration or malnutrition, is said to trigger variegation. Ecological disturbance by fire, flood, frosts, hurricanes, drought or predatory fauna where the plant is severely damaged are also claimed as possible causes. Some botantists believe plants in poor health are more prone to virus attack, effecting variegation. Fundamentally, leading authorities acknowledge gene mutations cause at least some variegations, viruses are singularly responsible for others, but both causes may interrelate elsewhere. A number of naturally striped species breed true seed (for example, *Tillandsia cyanea*), which confuses our concept of 'normal' and 'abnormal' plants.

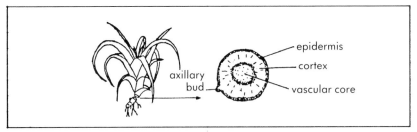

Figure 21   Cross-sectional view of a mature bromeliad stem

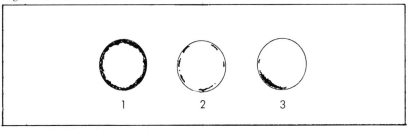

Figure 22   Types of variegation in cross-section (albinistic tissues or areas of reduced chloroplasts are represented in black): 1 periclinal chimera; 2 mericlinal chimera; 3 sectorial chimera.

Types of Variegation

Plants with two distinct types of tissue such as diploid/tetraploid or albinistic/chlorophyllous tissues are called chimeras. There are numerous genetic combinations but the definition as applied here refers to variegates only. Variegation may be fixed or unstable, and temporary or permanent, traits which are relative to their timespan under cultivation. A reduced number of chloroplasts (photosynthetic organelles containing chlorophyll) shows as lighter green or yellow tissues. A complete absence of chloroplasts produces albinistic tissue which is white or cream.

Figure 21 is a cross-sectional view of the stem of a mature bromeliad. This reveals three basic types of variegation, as simplified in Figure 22.

1. Periclinal chimera, where a thin ring of albinistic tissue surrounds the stem perimeter (epidermis) whilst the central vascular core is green. Pups or buds developing from this stem area duplicate the variegated pattern of the parent plant. If the variegation in this configuration mutates further or degenerates, pups will no longer be identical to the original.

2. Mericlinal chimera, where a small segmented layer of albinistic tissue is situated on or near the epidermis whilst nearly all cortex and vascular core tissues are green. Very limited variegation can occur in the total plant or in an offset from an axillary bud along the

stem. Whole leaves may be solid green and variegation appears inconsistently and is poorly defined.

3. Sectorial chimera, where the stem in cross-section has albinistic tissue in a confined area of the epidermis whilst the inner tissues are green. This wedged division of tissues produces both wholly green pups and regularly variegated pups.

Many of the most distinctive sports (bud mutants) or variegates derived from seed are periclinal chimeras. Nine visual forms of variegation are recognised botanical definitions (Figure 23), although their established application has not always been consistent and accurate. The term 'variegata' often implies any variegated form, which is misleading.

1. Marginata, usually albo-marginata, meaning white-edged; the central leaf zone remains solid green; for example, *Aechmea fulgens* var. *discolor* 'Albo-marginata'.
2. Variegata, with the leaf edge green and the middle portion white or yellow; for example, *Aechmea fasciata* cv. 'Variegata'.
3. Striata, where the foliage is green overlaid with longitudinal white or yellow stripes of varying widths; for example, *Nidularium innocentii* var. 'Roseastriata' is a pink-striped variant.
4. Lineatum, with the green leaf heavily overlaid with many fine lines; for example, *Nidularium innocentii* var. 'Rosea-lineata' is a pink-lined variant.
5. Medio-picta, meaning literally 'painted middle'; similar to the varie-

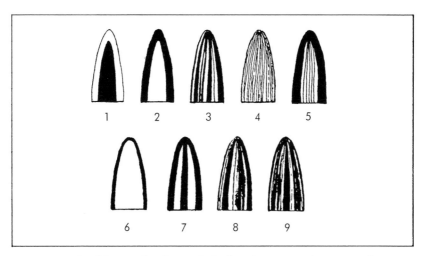

Figure 23   Visual forms of variegates in leaf section: 1 *marginata*; 2 *variegata*; 3 *striata*; 4 *lineatum*; 5 *medio-picta*; 6 *paxianum*; 7 *bivittatus*; 8 *tricolor*; 9 *quadricolor*.

gata form but green striations separate the central band; for example, *Aechmea lueddemanniana* 'Medio-picta'.

6. Paxianum, with green leaf margins and a single, broad median white stripe; for example, *Nidularium innocentii* var. *paxianum*.
7. Bivittatus, meaning literally double striped lengthwise; two central bands of cream or pink on the green leaf; for example, *Cryptanthus bivittatus*.
8. Tricolor, 'of three colours', usually green, cream and pink; for example, *Cryptanthus bromelioides* var. *tricolor*.
9. Quadricolor, 'of four colours', usually white, yellow, red and green; for example, *Aechmea magdalenae* var. *quadricolor*.

The forms tricolor and quadricolor are loosely used to describe an inflorescence also, or in conjunction with the foliage.

From the above descriptions many versions, particularly in the marginata, variegata and striata forms grown nowadays, appear to be no longer true to name. Probably they have deviated by degrees or mutated further from the original clone through additional lines or displacement of zones. However, reclassifying such offspring would be difficult with this constantly variable factor. Sometimes sports from the same species or hybrids arise independently in separate localities and are named identically. The two clones may differ considerably in quality, growth habits and appearance, of which the potential grower or buyer should be well aware. For instance, one clone of *Aechmea fasciata* 'Albo-marginata', no matter how well grown, has faded variegation at maturity, whereas another clone holds the colour. Conversely, some variegates sold under different names in fact represent the same plant. For example, *Guzmania zahnii* 'Omer Morobe' is known also as the forms *variegata* and *tricolor*. Another aspect of incorrect nomenclature is that botanical varieties were originally found in the wild whereas cultivars are not, unless as 'escapees' from cultivation.

In accordance with the current International Rules of Botanical Nomenclature, numerous recent variegates have been named in modern language but unfortunately do not describe the variegation; for example, *Aechmea apocalyptica* 'Helen Dexter', *Aechmea nudicaulis* 'Mary Hyde', *Cryptanthus fosterianus* 'Elaine', *Aechmea chantinii* 'Samurai' and *Aechmea lueddemanniana* 'Mend'.

The red pigment anthocyanin is present in many bromeliads, and located in the epidermal cells overlying both chlorophyllous and albinistic tissues. Where variegation transverses a species' crossband or blotches, as in *Aechmea orlandiana* 'Ensign', anthocyanins may duplicate the pattern in albinistic tissue with red or pink. Variegation in highly scurfed species, such as *Tillandsia xerographica* forma *variegata*, is often not seen to advantage unless wet. Rosa-lineata and rosea-striata forms feature in discolor foliage variegates, and are more prominent on the leaf reverse.

Brown striped variegates have occurred in several hybrids, such as *Aechmea* 'Electra striata' and *Neoregelia* 'Amazing Grace'. Variegation sometimes appears only at the apex of leaf blades, as in *Vriesea platynema* var. *variegata*. It is interesting to note spines and leaf bracts seldom change colour in variegates. Occasionally variegation extends into the inflorescence; *Tillandsia viridiflora* var. *variegata* and *Guzmania lingulata* 'Broadview' variegata both have striped scape bracts. Whether variegation appears on both upper and lower leaf surfaces depends on the chimeral type, individual leaf thickness and location of the albinistic tissue in the mesophyll (green chlorophyll) tissue. The visible distinction between colour zones ranges from the precise sharpness of *Aechmea ornata* var. *nationalis* to the gradual suffusion of *Cryptanthus* × 'Glad' (Foster's No. 2 Hybrid).

Propagation

In theory, offspring multiplied by asexual (vegetative) reproduction ought to duplicate the parent but this basic method is obviously not always reliable for variegates. Even the best of so-called fixed clones mutate occasionally but some, such as *Aechmea coelestis* var. *albomarginata* and *Ananas bracteatus* var. *tricolor*, have remained consistent generation after generation for decades.

As a rule the highly variegated chimeras are weaker in growth than their green counterparts. Smaller rosettes and inflorescences than usual are formed, with less propensity to offset. Some variegates are notoriously slow-growing, particularly vrieseas and guzmanias, and can be difficult to root. For all types, it is best to leave pups attached longer than usual—greed and impatience are not always rewarded. From experience, offsets one-third to one-half the parent's size are safe to separate but sprouting of adventitious roots on the attached pup is the best guide. With stoloniferous types such as *Aechmea* 'Foster's Favorite' and *Nidularium billbergioides* 'variegatum', it is an advantage to aerial layer the offsets to minimise any setback. To propagate stock numbers quicker, removing the inflorescence, once formed, is recommended so energy is channelled into offsets, not flowers and seeds. Incising the growing point of near-mature rosettes with a sharp knife has the same effect.

Unstable variegates tend to throw albino or totally green pups. True albinos (no chlorophyll) eventually die even if left on the parent stock so should be removed once detected. Pseudo-albino pups, where a uniform yellow-green occurs, can mature. For instance, *Billbergia* × 'Santa Barbara' and *Billbergia pyramidalis* 'Striata' feature this reduction in chlorophyll but still multiply satisfactorily.

By observing the leaf markings and overall foliage pattern the grower can spot any tendency to mutate. If single leaves or a foliage section has disproportionate colour bands for its form, probably the clone is degenerating or sprouting further. Where the change is immediate, drastic action may save the chimera as total albinism spells death to the plant. One proven technique is to remove all inferior pups until the parent produces an offset directly below a well-marked leaf sheath as this is more likely to retain the desired characteristics. However, in less vigorous cultivars the grower may have to forego this puritanical approach if the right pup seems unlikely to emerge within the parent's life span. A classic example of instability is *Neoregelia carolinae* 'meyendorfii variegata' from which as many as ten different sports may arise in one generation of pups. The two contrasting forms of *Aechmea caudata* var. 'Variegata' illustrate this divergence also.

Many superb variegates originated as chance seedlings from plain green species as with *Aechmea lindenii* var. *makoyana*. Ironically, seed from self-pollinated variegates seldom breed true, reverting back to the type plant. One noted exception is *Neoregelia carolinae* 'Meyendorfii albomarginata' whose variegated seedlings may be up to 20 per cent of the batch raised. Germinating albino seedlings soon perish once the starch reserves of the seed are exhausted. Increasing variegates by tissue culture has had limited success, largely due to separation of the chimeral components. On average 30 to 40 per cent of tissues stay variegated but seldom are they the quality of the cloned plant. One exceptional 'happy accident' was the meristem inversion of *Cryptanthus* 'It' to produce *Cryptanthus* 'Ti'. Usually 3 to 5 per cent of all bromeliad meristem cultures produce variegates but they are of very poor quality.

General Care

Variegates range from the tough *Aechmea bracteata* 'Variegata' to the soft *Guzmania musaica* 'Variegata' but generally need more attention and care than conventional bromeliads for best results. Robust specimens like *Bromelia serra* forma *variegata* and the scarcer *Bromelia balansae* forma *tricolor* are easier to grow than other variegated forms. Conversely, items like *Vriesea splendens* var. *striatifolia* and *Vriesea ensiformis* var. *striata* require extra pampering to keep the leaves in good condition.

Cultivars and species of the albo-marginata form in particular are prone to cold burn of the leaf edges and crown rot in low winter temperatures. In summer lack of humidity shows in lack-lustre foliage and leaf-tip dieback, an ailment corrected by regular misting. Good ventilation is doubly essential for variegates as closed, stuffy or over-crowded conditions suit pests—various types of scale—to which they are susceptible. Malathion sprayed at half strength will give control and prevent these sap-suckers from disfiguring the plant.

Broadly speaking variegates need as much if not more light than conventional bromeliads to retain the leaf patterns. Less then optimal light can cause a greening of the variegation, wholly or partially, to produce more chlorophyll. Loss of pink or bronze tones is the warning signal although seasonal effects have some bearing. Too intense a light can bleach or yellow the contrasting colours, as happens with *Billbergia pyramidalis* cv. *striata*. Similarly, pinking of *Billbergia* × 'Santa Barbara' reduces the pattern but personal preference will help dictate the conditions preferred.

It is claimed variegates absorb less water and nutrients than other bromeliads. Considering their generally reduced vitality due to loss of food-manufacturing chlorophyll, this supposition bears credence. However, unless variegates are segregated, a separate watering programme may be impractical in a mixed collection. Some growers maintain variegates produce the best markings when kept slightly hungry. An overdose of nitrogen in particular can cause greening of white or yellow tissues, which may be irreversible with unstable variegates. Where overfed, repotting into a poorer potting medium may solve the situation if light or genetic factors are not involved. Many epiphytic variegates are sparse-rooting so extra crocking and even staking may be necessary. Some variegates' foliage develops necrotic spots (dead brown patches) with age, a condition for which there is no known cure as a benign virus is believed responsible. Variegation in some varieties or cultivars fades at maturity, either in the inner leaf blades or outer apices. It is suspected a hormonal imbalance may be involved, possibly in conjunction with cultural or genetic factors.

Malformation

Distortions such as fasciation, dwarfism, gigantism, etc. are prevalent in plants and bromeliad variegates have their peculiarities too. Misshapen, stunted, fused and quilled leaves are not uncommon features. A tendency to partial or complete sterility is noted in hybrid variegates in particular. In extreme cases intermittent flowering, or non-flowering, can occur. An example is the non-flowering form of *Neoregelia carolinae* 'Tricolor' listed commercially as 'spiralis'. Its contorted manner of leaf blade placement certainly suggests a curious mixture of genes. The Australian hybrid × *Neobergia* (*Neoregelia carolinae* forma *tricolor* × *Billbergia nutans*) was once thought to exhibit aneuploidy (characterised by an inability to mature) but in several instances an inflorescence has formed. Its strange, reed-like growth with faint banding shows the difficulties of mixing compatible genes from different genera. Impaired fertility may arise where variegates are cross-bred; *Cryptanthus* 'It' as a pollen parent contributes some of its characteristics to the progeny but as a seed parent produces all albino seedlings. Aborted offsets can occur where the variety or cultivar lacks vigour to support several pups to maturity simultaneously.

Summary

As shown by the previous sections, the fascinating study of bromeliad variegation is technically complex and unravelling all its mysteries may be a long-term scientific goal. Variegates may always be regarded as the 'weak-freaks' of the family, by scientists. However, the ideal side-benefit for growers from such research would be easier control or manipulation in cultivation. Because of their inherent problems, variegates provide an extra challenge for horticulturists to achieve the ultimate in outstanding foliage plants. Bizarrely marked variegates from 'touchy' species have proved difficult to keep alive even with the best care. One gem to suffer the fate of extinction was the marginata form of *Vriesea hieroglyphica* known as 'Madame Morobe'. The remarkable phenomenon of variegation is that such a clone can emerge again at any time, so perhaps it is not lost forever.

As in any field there are the 'beginner's dozen' which the average collector can grow and enjoy without much trouble—the universally popular *Neoregelia carolinae* forma *tricolor* surely leads the way. Other easy, prolific types to try include *Billbergia* × 'Santa Barbara' and *Billbergia pyramidalis* 'Striata'. Maybe the rarer, valuable and perhaps more ornamental types with their demanding habits are better left to the specialist with the expertise and facilities to succeed. The best advice could be to grow the type plant well first before attempting its variegated form.

Wherever variegates are displayed, their striking, exotic appearance always attracts attention and admiration. To produce a variegate clump in full bloom truly is a worthy ambition for many growers.

BROMELIAD SOCIETIES

For growers of any unique types of plants, such as bromeliads, there are many advantages in belonging to a group which specialises in their culture. By meeting or corresponding with like-minded individuals, plants and knowledge can be freely interchanged. There are societies based in many parts of the world and hopes are high that the British Bromeliad Society will be reformed once again. Anyone who is interested in becoming a potential member of the society should write to: Mr R.S. Houghton, 16 Culcheth Hall Drive, Culcheth, Warrington, Cheshire WA3 4PS.

Major societies in other parts of the world include:

The American Bromeliad Society Inc., 2488 East 49, Tulsa, Oklahoma 74015, USA.

The Bromeliad Society of Australia Inc., PO Box 340, Ryde, New South Wales 2112, Australia.

BROMELIAD NURSERIES

UK and European nurseries

Anmore Exotics, the George Staunton Estate, Petersfield Road, Havant, Hants PO9 5HB

Hollygate Nurseries, Ashington, West Sussex RH20 3BA

Mallorn Gardens, Lanner Hill, Redruth, Cornwall TR16 6DA

Vesutor Ltd, Marringdean Rd, Billingshurst, West Sussex RH14 9EH

B. Wall, 4 Selbourne Close, New Haw, Weybridge, Surrey KT15 3RG

A Schenkel, 2 Hamburg 55 — Blankenese, West Germany (seed)

United States nurseries

Beach Garden Nursery, PO Box 697, Delhi, CA 95315

Bromeliad Brokers, PO Box 435, Washingtonville, NU 10992

Claire's Bromeliads, 720 Balour Drive, Encinitas, CA 92024

Cornelison Bromeliads, 225 San Bernardino Street, N. Fort Myers, FL 33903

Dana Co., 4626 Lamont, Corpus Christi, TX 78411

De Leon's Bromeliad World, 8880 S.W. 80th Street, Miami, FL 33173

His 'n' Hers Bromeliad Nursery, 2112 W. Carol Drive, Fullerton, CA 92633

Jery Hoernig, 3228 Gerle Avenue, Placerville, CA 95667

Kent's Bromeliad Nursery, 703 Pomelo Drive, Vista, CA 92083

Marilynn's Garden, 13421 Sussex Place, Santa Ana, CA 92705

Marz Bromeliads, 10782 Citrus Drive, Moorpark, CA 93021

M. Oppenheimer Bromeliads, PO Box 960, San Antonio, TX 78284

Plant Ranch, 2020 Tweed Street, Placentia, CA 92670

W.K. Quality Bromeliads, PO Box 49621, Los Angeles, CA 90049

FURTHER READING

BENZING, DAVID H *The Biology of the Bromeliads*. Eureka, California: Mad River Press, 1980.

BROMELIAD SOCIETY INC. *A Bromeliad Glossary*. Arcadia, California: Kerr Printing, 1977.

BROMELIAD SOCIETY INC. *Bromeliads, a Cultural Handbook*. Arcadia, California: Kerr Printing, 1953.

BROMELIAD SOCIETY INC. BSI Journals. Editor, 1508 Lake Shore Drive, Orlando, Florida. (Six issues per year).

HANSON, BEA. *Bromeliads for everyone*. Auckland, New Zealand: Business Printing Works, 1970.

INNES, CLIVE. *Air-plants and other Bromeliads*. Exeter: Justin Knowles Publishing Group, 1990.

ISLEY III, PAUL T. *Genus Tillandsia*. Gardena, California: Paul T. Isley III, 1977.

ISLEY III, PAUL T. *Tillandsia*. Gardena, California: Botanical Press, 1987.

KRAMER, JACK. *Bromeliads*. New York: Harper & Row, 1981.

LEA, TONY. *The Beauty of Bromeliads*. Caloundra, Queensland: Taralkon, 1984.

PADILLA, VICTORIA. *Bromeliads*. New York: Crown Publishers, 1973.

PADILLA VICTORIA. *The Colourful Bromeliads*. Arcadia, California: Kerr Printing, 1981.

RAUH, WERNER. *Bromeliads for Home, Garden and Greenhouse*. Dorset, UK: Blandford Press, 1979.

READ, M. 'Bromeliads threatened by trade'. *Kew Magazine* 6(1): 22–9, 1989.

RICHTER, WALTER. *Bromeliads*. Arcadia, California: Kerr Printing, 1977.

RODRIGUEZ, A. 'Living on air'. *The Garden* 114(9): 444–8, 1989.

SEABORN, BILL. *Bromeliads*. Laguna Hills, California: Gick Publishing, 1976.

WILSON, LOUIS. *Bromeliads for modern living*. Kalamazoo, Michigan: Merchants Publishing, 1977.

LIST OF GENERA

Bromelioideae
Acanthostachys
Aechmea
Ananas
Andrea
Androlepis
Araeococcus
Billbergia
Bromelia
Canistrum
Cryptanthus
Disteganthus
Fascicularia
Fernseea
Greigia
Hohenbergia
Hohenbergiopsis

Neoglaziovia
Neoregelia
Nidularium
Ochagavia
Orthophytum
Portea
Pseudananas
Quesnelia
Ronnbergia
Streptocalyx
Wittrockia

Pitcairnioideae
Abromeitiella
Ayensua
Brocchinia
Connellia

Cottendorfia
Deuterocohnia
Dyckia
Encholirium
Fosterella
Hechtia
Navia
Pitcairnia
Puya

Tillandsioideae
Catopsis
Glomeropitcairnia
Guzmania
Mezobromelia
Tillandsia
Vriesea

GLOSSARY

Abortive Undeveloped, defective, barren.

Acantha Spine, thorn.

Acute Tapering to a sharp point.

Albino Plants that have white floral bracts and flowers, although normally they would be coloured. Albino seedlings are pure white.

Ampule Bottle- or urn-shaped.

Analogue Similar.

Angiosperm A plant with seeds enclosed in an ovary.

Anterior Facing away from the axis.

Anther The top of the stamen, the pollen-bearing part of a flower.

Anthesis When the flower is fully open, the flowering period when the pollen is ripe.

Anthocyanin Blue, violet or red pigment which affects colour in the Bromeliaceae.

Apical At the growing tip or apex.

Apice Growing tip or apex.

Apiculate Ending abruptly in a little point.

Appendage A secondary part or attached subsidiary.

Asexual Without sex, sexless.

Atmospheric Plants that live exclusively from humidity of the air.

Axil The juncture of leaf and stem.

Axis The main stem or central part about which organs or branches are arranged.

Baccate Having berry-like seeds, soft and fleshy.

Banded Marked with crossbands and horizontal lines of a different colour.

Bicaudate Having two tail-like appendages.

Bicolor Having two colours.

Bigeneric A cross between species of different genera.

Biota The plant and animal life of a particular region.

Bisexual Flowers which have both male and female parts.

Blade The expanded part of a leaf.

Bract A leaflike plant part, sometimes brightly coloured and located below a flower or on the stalk of a flower cluster.

Calyx The outer protective covering of a flower.

Capsule The seed pod, a dry fruit which eventually splits open to shed the seeds.

Caudate Having a tail or a tail-like part.

Caudex A woody, trunk-like stem.

143

Caulescent Having a stem above the ground.

Characteristic A distinguishing quality or trait.

Chimera Plant tissues of different genetic constitution in the same part of the plant often resulting in variegation.

Chloroplast A minute granule containing chlorophyll, developed only in cells exposed to light. Chloroplasts are the centre of starch formation.

Chlorophyll The green pigment in plants.

Chromosome One of the gene-carrying bodies in the tissue of a cell before division. It contains the genes that convey hereditary characteristics.

Clone A plant raised from a single cell, or derived vegetatively from one specimen.

Coma A tuft of hair, as on some seeds.

Compound A branching inflorescence. Having two or more similar parts in one organ.

Concolor Having only one colour.

Connate United or joined together.

Corolla The inner row of floral parts, composed of petals.

Cotyledon The primary leaf in the embryo.

Crown Where the base of the plant joins the root.

Cultivar A plant produced or evolved in cultivation.

Cusp A pointed end.

Cyathiforme Cup-shaped.

Deciduous Losing leaves at certain times.

Digitate Finger-like, with members arising from one point.

Dioecious Male and female flowers borne on separate plants.

Diploid Having the normal complement of two similar sets of chromosomes.

Discolor Having two different colours.

Distichous Having two rows of leaves or flowers, as in some vrieseas.

DNA Deoxyribonucleic acid, the main constituent of the chromosomes of all organisms. It is responsible for the transmission of hereditary characteristics.

Ecology The set of relationships between organisms and environment.

Embryo A plant in the early stages of development, within the seed.

Endosperm The tissue which is enclosed in the embryo of the seed and serves to nourish it when germinating.

Enzyme Any of a group of complex proteins produced by living cells, that act as catalysts in specific biochemical reactions.

Epidermal Relating to the protective covering of a plant, or plant part.

Epiphyte A plant that attaches itself to another plant or object to grow, but is not a parasite.

Exserted Projecting, as stamens from a perianth.

Farinose Covered with mealy powder.

Fasciation A distortion caused by several stems becoming fused into one.

Fasciculate Clusters of flowers, closely growing.

Fenestralis The light green rectangular areas on the leaves, which give the illusion of windows.

Fertile Capable of producing pollen, seeds or fruit.

Filament Stalk of an anther.

Foliar Referring to leaves, foliage.

Fungicide A material that kills fungi.

Furfuraceous Covered with scales or scurf.

Fusiform Spindle-shaped.

Gamete Either male or female sex cell.

Gene The part of a chromosome which determines hereditary characteristics.

Genus A group of related species.

Germination The growth of a seed into a plantlet.

Glabrous Without scales or hairs, glossy, smooth.

Glaucous Covered with a fine, whitish, powdery coating—sea-greenish.

Globose Globe-shaped.

Habitat The locality in which a plant normally grows.

Haploid Having a single set of unpaired chromosomes.

Herbaceous With fleshy stems, not woody.

Hetero More than one kind.

Homo One of a kind.

Hormone Organic compound produced by a plant, essential for growth.

Hybrid A plant developed by taking pollen from one plant and depositing it on the stigma of another plant, either of the same or a different genus.

Imbricate Overlapping.

Inflorescence The part of the plant that holds the flower or flower cluster.

Intercalary Between the apex and the base.

Internode The part of a stem between two nodes or joints.

Lanceolate Widening above the base and tapering to a point, lance-shaped.

Lateral From the side, as an inflorescence growing from the side of a plant, rather than the centre.

Lax Loose, open, not compact.

Lepidote Covered with small scales.

Meristem The growing tissue at the tips of roots and at the apex of vegetative or floral shoots.

Mesophyll Tissue of the leaf which is vital.

Metabolism Chemical activity that occurs in living organisms, resulting in growth, production of energy for vital processes, etc.

Monocarp Flowers or fruits only once.

Monocotyledon A plant, characterised in the main by producing seeds of a single cotyledon or seed leaf.

Monoecious Having male and female flowers on the same plant.

Monotypic Represented by a single member.

Mucro A sharp and short tip.

Mutagen A substance that can

induce genetic mutation.

Mutation A change in chromosome or gene.

Nectar The sugary secretion of a plant.

Nematodes Unsegmented worms with tough outer cuticles.

Node A swollen or knoblike structure, a joint where a leaf may be borne.

Nomenclature A system of naming, an international code designed for universal comprehension.

Nutrient A substance or chemical needed for growth.

Obtuse Rounded at the end, blunt.

Offset A shoot that develops laterally at the base of a plant, which may produce another plant, a pup or offshoot.

Ovary The part of the pistil containing the seed.

Ovule A small egg, a rudimentary seed of a plant.

Organelle A structural and functional unit in a cell.

Panicle A loosely and irregularly branched flower cluster.

Paniculate Arranged, or growing in a panicle.

Pathogen An organism which produces disease.

Pedicel A small stem serving as a support for a single flower.

Pendent (also pendant). Hanging down from its support.

Perianth The outer envelope of a flower, consisting of calyx and corolla (sepals and petals respectively).

Perennial Having a life cycle of more than two seasons.

Petal A separate, often coloured segment of a corolla.

Petiole A leaf stalk.

Photosynthesis The process by which plants capture the sun's energy and convert it into chemical energy. The formation of carbohydrates from water and the carbon dioxide of the air, in the chlorophyll-containing tissues of plants exposed to light.

Pistil Female organ of a flower, including ovary, style and stigma.

Pollen The fertilising dust of a flower.

Polystichous Arranged in rows, with branches radiating from the axis.

Pup A vegetative offset arising from the rootstock or from creeping stems.

Quilling A condition found in offsets in which the centre leaves form a tight roll. They are stuck to each other by a glutinous substance.

Raceme An inflorescence bearing flowers on short stems in succession toward the axis.

Rhizome A root-bearing stem which travels underground and sends up leafy shoots.

Rosette A circular cluster of leaves radiating from a crown.

Saxicolous Growing on rocks.

Scale Minute, flat, absorbing organs through which many bromeliads obtain their nutrients. Also a small sucking insect.

Scape Stem of the inflorescence, usually extending beyond the leaves.

146

Scurf Scale-like plates.

Seed The ripened ovule.

Self-fertilisation The transference of pollen from an anther to the stigma of the same flower.

Sepal The flower parts which surround or contain the petals.

Sessile The flower rests directly on the stem, not stalked.

Sheath The flattened covering which protects the developing inflorescence.

Simple A single, unbranched inflorescence.

Spathe A stiff, leathery bract enclosing an inflorescence.

Species A group of plants which have in common one or more characteristics which separate it from any other group.

Spike An inflorescence with stalkless or short-stalked flowers borne on an erect, unbranched flower stem.

Sport A mutation, a sudden deviation from typical form.

Stamen The pollen-bearing male organ of a flower.

Sterile Barren.

Stigma The female portion of a flower which receives pollen from the anther.

Stolon Long sucker or runner, that forms a new plant at its tip.

Stomata Breathing pores in the leaves of plants.

Style The elongated part of the pistil between the ovary and the stigma.

Substrate The medium upon which a plant or seed grows.

Tank A water-filled cup-like depression formed, in the centre of many bromeliads, from overlapping leaves.

Taxonomy The science concerned with the classification of organisms into groups based on similarities of structure and origin.

Terrestrial Growing in the ground.

Tetraploid An organism having four sets of chromosomes, which is twice the normal number.

Translucent Partially transparent.

Trichome The scale found on the leaves of most bromeliads, the minute, absorbing organs through which nutrients are obtained.

Tufted Having a cluster of hairs.

Unisexual Flowers of one sex only.

Variegation A leaf which has pale stripes, bands or blotches because certain sections have reduced, or are totally devoid of green pigments.

Variety A plant with slight differences from the type of the species.

Vascular With ducts or vessels.

Vegetative reproduction Reproduction by means of offshoots.

Viability The possibility for growth, such as the germination of seed.

Virus A sub-microscopic particle which causes disease.

Whorl Three or more flowers or leaves at one node.

Woolly Has long, soft, matted hairs resembling wool.

Xerophyte A plant which survives under arid conditions.

INDEX